Ellen Sidaway who was born Ellen ⌐ [barcode: CW00386409] on 3rd June 1914. This is her life stor̄ she was 82. It was two years in the ᵥ love story that has lasted all her life. Ellen went to school in the 1920s; work and marriage in the 1930s; the war and austerity of the 1940s; Hope and set backs in the 1950s; motoring adventures in the 1960; set backs again in the 1970s and coming to terms with life alone in the 1980s. Twenty years on from writing her Memoirs and Ellen is fine and well. She is not as mobile as she would like, she has reduced hearing and her eyes are now failing her but she is mentally alert. One of her redeeming qualities is that everybody who visits her leave with a smile on their face as she relates even more incidents of her life. Since writing this book she has had another life but sadly that will never be written.

Tears have been shed in happiness and sadness; she saw good times and bad; births, marriages and deaths of friends and relatives. It's called life and Ellen had a full life. I hope that you enjoy reading my Mother's memoirs.

Colin Sidaway May 2017

The Memoirs of Ellen Sidaway

C. S. SIDAWAY

SIDAWAY PUBLICATIONS LTD

The Memoirs of Ellen Sidaway

© C. S. Sidaway 2017

Published in 2017
by Sidaway Publications Ltd
www.colsbostinbooks.co.uk

The moral right of the author has been asserted according to
the Copyright, Designs and Patents Act 1988.

A catalogue card for this book is available from the British Library.

Paperback ISBN: 978-0-9955472-6-1
Ebook ISBN: 978-0-9955472-7-8

Printed and bound by TJ International, Cornwall, UK

INTRODUCTION

HOW THE BOOK CAME TO BE WRITTEN

I found that Mother was always good at telling anecdotes going back to her early childhood. She always seemed to put a humorous spin on what were quite ordinary and mundane everyday events. In her 80's she was incapacitated and in great pain from Sciatica and Arthritis. It happed at Christmas time and she describes that in her Memoirs and spent three weeks in respite. When she arrived back home she thought that she wouldn't be able to cope. In just a short time she had become institutionalised.

I gave Ellen a notepad and pen telling her to put her life story down and to my surprise she did! It took her two years to complete. She had interruptions as people asked to read the next chapter as it was written. At each stage Ellen more or less had to repeat those events. Upon reading the text there are some sections that are out of sequence as she probably remembered something that she had overlooked and just continued writing. It doesn't detract from her story. She wrote it as she would tell her story.

When she had completed the hand written version I made 20 photocopies that I bound and gave to family and friends. I put a copy into the Lye Library and I managed to keep a copy. Ellen still has the original. Her memoirs lay in my desk draw almost forgotten until my friend Colin Macdonald picked up her story. This came about as he had put some photographs on a web site, www.stourbridge.com and I saw a photograph of 3 Cross Walks and also 3 The Dock. I wanted to print copies and made contact with Colin. He became interested in

Ellen's story. I scanned my copy of the manuscript and he typed it up and put it on the Black Country Living Museum web site.

Since writing her Memories, nearly 20 years have passed. She still bright and alert although age is taking its toll on her physically. She will celebrate her 103rd birthday this year. This printed copy will be a fitting tribute to a lovely lady. If I have a regret and that is that I didn't get her to read and record the text of the book. It is written as she would tell the story. It is not sanitised Oxford English but a true Lye, Black Country dialect that is grammatically incorrect with the occasional descriptive word that is not in any dictionary. I also wanted to also show her hand writing that she was taught nearly a century ago but we have to settle for typescript.

Colin Sidaway. May 2017.

IN THE BEGINNING – 1914

My mother's husband died young, leaving her with two boys, Fred and Stan. She married again, and I came along. I was born at 143 Hay Green Lye, a small house just two rooms up and two down, facing Lye football ground. Fred was fourteen years old and Stan eleven years. Fred worked down the pit at Oldnall Colliery and when Stan was thirteen he went to work in the pit bank. Mother had to be up at six o clock to get the fire going to boil the kettle, and cook the bacon for the lads to take with them. We had no stove, everything had to be cooked over the fire. Stan was a terror to get up in a morning, and having to keep calling him always woke me. I would creep downstairs, Mom would give me a piece of bread dipped in the bacon fat, and make me sit up the corner by the fire until the lads had gone to work. That was my earliest memory.

I started at Stambermill School when I was three years old. Every Monday morning we had to march into Stambermill Church for a one hour service. My mother went to work at a brick yard at Hay Green which was quite near the school, and during our lunch time break, twelve noon till two pm I would go to her. The places where the women worked were called STOWS. It was quite warm inside, they wore large calico aprons and bare feet, why I don't know, but to me it was fascinating to see them making bricks.

Saturday night was bath night for me, in a little tin bath in front of the fire. I had long hair, and mother would put it in rags, next morning I had long ringlets, and I used to go to the cottage next door to show the old couple my lovely hair. So much for my early memories.

When a little older, I went to Sunday School and I remember going to Habberley Valley in Samuel Johnson's coach, it was a big open thing with no top. This was our Sunday School treat, when we got there, we were all excited and started to run down the valley. I fell and grazed my knee, but that didn't prevent me from winning the next race. My prize was a printing set which I kept for years. Sunday mornings I would be around five years old, mother made me visit my relatives on my Dad's side. There was my Aunt Alice in Summer Street, Aunt Ellen in Belmont Road, Aunt Leah on Waste Bank, and Aunt Donnie who lived on top of Waste Bank. She was my favourite, not having any children, they made a fuss of me. She kept a little shop at the front of the house, made and sold her own bread. The Sunday joint was cooked in front of the fire, the meat tin was placed on top of a big biscuit tin, and the meat was attached to a large hook, which she turned and basted as it cooked. I often stayed to dinner and sometimes to tea, when the best china tea set would be laid out, (something my mother didn't possess) and when I was ready to go home, Uncle Ben would give me a penny, and Aunt Donnie would give me some sweets all screwed up in newspaper. I loved to go to my Aunt Donnies.

Every year there was a horse fair at Bromsgrove and Fred decided to go, there was no transport and he had to walk all the way, and he came back with a horse. He put me on its back and off we went to show our Gran who lived in Engine Lane. Mom was mad, what to do with a horse. The first night he tied it to some railings around our house, what happened to it afterwards I can't remember, he probably sold it. My Gran was getting old and frail, and she had two unmarried sons living with her, Noah and Steve, and Mom was finding it too much for her to run two homes. I was eight years old when we left Hay Green and moved to Engine Lane to live with Gran. We were overcrowded, but somehow we coped. My old gran could neither read or write as she had never been to school. Although we had gas lights Gran would never use it, always kept to her large oil lamp in the middle of the table. I remember reading a book to her called Uncle Tom's cabin, she had a good memory and would always tell me where I had left off. It helped to pass our winter evenings.

Fred left the coal mine and started buying and selling dogs, mostly puppies. At the bottom of the garded there were two pigsties, Uncle Steve looked after the pigs, my Dad had pigeons in a large pen, and Fred kept the dogs in a large shed with a stable door, while waiting to be sold. He would advertise them in a paper called "Our dogs" and send them all over the country. My job was to go up Lye and buy crates from any of the shops which he would make into little boxes for the puppies and I would carry them to the station to catch the 8pm train. Animals always had to travel by night. They always had a good meal and water before being dispatched.

Mom had left the brickyard, Monday was washday, she had to light the fire under the cast iron boiler to get the water hot, everything was rubbed out in a tin bath in the sink, then into the dolly tub and given a good dollying, then through a good old mangle, and into the boiler. From there they were rinsed and whites put through a blue water, and then all shirt collars, tablecloths and pillow cases were starched, and although mom paid the woman next door to help her, it seemed to take all day. The boiler was thoroughly cleaned out, and next day Uncle Steve boiled a sack of potatoes for the pigs, cleaned out again and Wednesday he brewed the beer. Always two barrels of beer in the pantry. My job was to fetch two penny worth of balm from a brewery in Pedmore Road, and an enamel jug full of finings from Harry Homsey's in Lye, these were used to make the beer.

Every year at the beginning of November the fair would come to Lye known as Lye Wake, most exciting event of the year. Late one Saturday night Uncle Noah went round the fair and won a big doll for me on the Chair-o-plane stall. I was in bed asleep but he came back and woke me up, he couldn't wait till morning. It was the only doll I ever had and I treasured it. In later years Mom persuaded me to give it to a little girl who was dying from consumption, so I said goodbye to my doll.

Fred did well selling dogs, and with his savings bought an old car, and learnt himself to drive. Uncle Noah had a lady friend named Lucy who lived in Kidderminster and one Sunday Fred said, come on Gran, who hadn't been out for years, didn't possess a coat, but in a tin trunk upstairs, Mom found her old Melton cloth cape and her Edwardian bonnet. Mom dressed her up and away we went in the old jalopy. I sat in the back with Gran, Uncle Noah and Fred in front. We thought we were royalty. Later on Fred had the car converted into a lorry, stopped selling dogs and went into the fruit and veg trade, and went around the streets of Stourbridge, hawking. The produce was delivered from Birmingham wholesale market. Apples came in big barrels, individually wrapped in paper, and tomatoes in baskets of corn. I would help to unwrap and polish the apples with a clean cloth, tomatoes too, any bruised were put on one side and put in the swill tub for the pigs. He only sold the best.

I was eight years old when I went hop picking for the first time, Mom couldn't go, but her friend Mrs Dimmock offered to take me. We went to Wormington Court, Stoke Edith, near Hereford, and loved it. Down in the hop field, she would open her umbrella, dig it into the clay upside down, and when I had filled it with hops so many times, I was allowed to go and play. Twice a week a man came into the hop fields selling lardy cakes, we named him the lardy cake man. He would carry them in a large basket on his arm, and shout as loud as he could LARDY CAKES! And you had to get to him quick before he sold out. Mrs Dimmock always gave me a penny to buy one. I made friends with a boy named Joey Nicholas, we were exactly the same age on the same date June 3rd. There was a large shanty with a big open fireplace, if it rained we would all congregate in there, and if it had been a nice day a fire would be lit outside, we would keep the fires going, as this was the only way of cooking or boiling kettles. The farmer provided the coke. It was a rather isolated farm, no houses or pubs, everybody went to bed early as we had to be up at seven o clock and down the hop fields as early as possible. Saturday afternoons Joey and I had to fetch the lamp oil, from the one and only shop about a mile down the lane. It seemed like two miles to us, but it helped to pass the time, and left Joey's Mom and Mrs Dimmock time to do other chores. A mobile shop came to the farm twice a week, and eggs and milk we had from the farm. We were there for five weeks. On my return Mom got me transferred to Orchard Lane Girls School, a much nicer school and I was happy there. I made friends with several girls who lived in Caledonia, I will refer to them later.

Christmas was hectic at our house, a pig would be killed a week before by a proper butcher. All our neighbours would order a joint and Christmas Eve I had to deliver the meat and collect the money. I always hung up a sock, but what did I get? A new penny, nuts and some sweets, but this one Christmas I had a surprise, I had a new scooter, only to find a foot of snow had fallen during the night and I couldn't ride it. Fred bought a new gramophone and records, we had to lift the lid, place the record on the turntable, adjust the needle, close the lid and wind it up. Remember there was no radio or television in those days. My favourite record was "In a monastery garden" Fred and Stan bought their friends to listen to this novelty, that Christmas we had a house full of men. Mom didn't mind, having killed a pig, there was plenty of roast pork, barrels of beer in the pantry and music laid on there was no need to go to a pub.

Later in the year as the weather improved Mom decided I should start taking my Dad's dinner. He worked down a marl hole getting out clay for the bricks, for the brick yard on the Hayes. I would come from school, and while Mom was getting his dinner ready, I would go in the pantry, cut myself a piece of home made cake, and draw myself a small glass of beer. The dinner she put in a basin, tied it up in a large red and white spotted handkerchief and I would tie it on the handlebars of my scooter and away I'd go. Now to get down to the bottom of the marl hole was very tricky, just a narrow path down a steep incline. I always rode down keeping one foot on the back wheel to steady myself. Dad and his mate would stop work and watch me, probably wondering if I was going to make it, but I never had any mishaps.

We seemed to have long hot summers and all my free time I spent up Caledonia with my school friends. There was Hilda Allport, Irene and

Elsie Cartwright, Amy Gorden, Phylis Hayes, Winnie Carradine, Fred Edwards and Joey. I say up Caledonia because it's on a hill, there's a new estate built there now, but apart from a few houses and one pub it was all fields. On the side of the road was a big tree trunk, where they would sit and wait for me, from this point they could see me coming down Engine Lane. Fred gave me two pence every night for helping him and I would call at a shop in Dudley road and buy a quarter of sweets which I shared with my friends. There was an area known as the Jackass, where we would play hide and seek. At the bottom was the River Stour where we sometimes went to paddle, it was quite shallow, not dangerous. The lads would tie a rope around the lamp post, and we would take turns to swing round. They were gas lamps in the streets in those days. Then there was hay making time, the pranks we used to play it's a wonder the farmer ever got his rick built.

Every August Bank holiday they held a fete at Corbett Hospital. I had never been, or seen a firework display, so with Mom's consent I stayed out later to see the fireworks. I remember we climbed on top of a hill and had a wonderful view as they lit the night sky. The next year we all went to the fete. We had to walk there over the fields and we had to go through a tunnel. A murder had been committed there years before and it was known as the murder tunnel, it was a bit scary going through it in the daylight, but coming back it was pitch dark, we clung to each other and ran screaming our heads off. I never forgot that tunnel.

Saturday afternoons we would all meet up and go to the Vic picture house (cinema). Admission 1d special kids films and always a serial, ending in the most exciting part, so you couldn't wait to see what happened the next week. Joey always sat by me, and one Saturday it was our birthday and while waiting for the film to start, he took something from his coat pocket and gave it to me. It was a mirror on a stand, it was a birthday present he had bought for me, from Bill's, a little shop opposite the Vic and it had cost him 4d, all his week's pocket money. I kept it in my sewing box for years. His Gran lived in Caledonia and his Mom visited her every night, when she left we knew it was time to go home, and one night whil waiting for her we sat on the step of the Staffordshire House pub, singing "On mother Kelly's doorstep", very appropriate. On the way down the road he told his Mom, that when he grew up he would marry me, but that wasn't to be, when we were thirteen years old his family moved to Wolverhampton and that was the last I saw or heard of Joey.

September came round again and I went hop picking with Mrs Dimmock to Leigh Court. Everybody had a large tin trunk, they needed to be large to hold everything you had to take with you for your use. Two buckets, two pots, frying pan, kettle, teapot, cups, saucers, cutlery, bowl, plates, tea, sugar, tins of milk (fresh milk went sour too quick). Towels, pillow cases, bed clothes, plus our working clothes, plus strong high lace-up boots and mack's, not forgetting a very keen knife for cutting the vines in the hop fields. I carried my clean clothes and oddments in a cardboard suitcase. On arriving at Leigh Court station, large wagons drawn by shire horses would be waiting to take the hop picking boxes to the farm, farm labourers would load and unload them. It was a very large barn which we all had to share. When everyone had decided which part of the barn they were going to occupuy they would start making the beds, spreading out the straw to make a mattress, and filling the pillow cases. Next a cart, loaded with army blankets would arrive, each family would be allotted one pair, they made the beds warmer and softer to sleep in. Then the boxes would be brought in, placed at the foot of the bed and unpacking would commence. The tin trunk was used as your table, this was the routine every year.

As you entered the barn there was a place separated from the living quarters, known as the shanty, with a large fireplace, where cooking was done and kettles boiled. It was all very primitive and absolutely no privacy, but everyone got on well together and I can't remember there being any dispute between them. Of course we were in the hop fields all day, weather permitting, Saturdays we finished at twelve o clock. I loved the weekends, I was never without a friend, we would go scrumping in the orchards, or walking down the lanes looking for filbert nuts in the hedgerows, we even found wild strawberries in the old Church yard. Fred got rid of his old car and bought a new Chevrolet lorry, and during the hop season he would go hawking around the Herefordshire farms.

On Friday nights on his way home he would call to see me, and give me all the sweets he hadn't sold. He would beg me to go home with him, but no, I was happy to stay. Mrs Dimmock was very good to me, and she must have liked my company, as she took me every year until I left school.

The next year new huts had been built for us, in a field just down the lane. So after my month's holiday it was back to school, in those days you had a choice whether you wanted to take the exam to go to technical college or not, and I declined, for one thing I didn't want to go in for teaching, and I didn't think My mother would want the expense of the uniforms if I had passed. However I must have been on the bright side, as they moved me from standard four into standard six, which was the top class. I sat on the back row next to the piano, on which was a large brass bell, and at playtime and lunchtime I had to go into the cloakroom and ring it as hard as I could. The Headmistress shared our classroom, sat at a large desk at the back of the room, so we all had to be on our best behaviour. During my last term I had to make two nightdresses for her, a pale pink and a pale blue, ankle length and long sleeves, every seam filled and done by hand. But I loved sewingand she was very pleased with my handiwork.

I finished school on my fourteenth birthday, the next day I went on a school outing to Rhyl, we went by train and it was the first time I had seen the sea, and on the following Monday I started work. Fred had a lady friend named Edith, whom he later married and she got me my job at Fawcetts sewing factory, in Allison Street, Digbeth, Birmingham.

I had to do six months apprenticeship at five shillings a week, six days a week, for we had to work Saturday mornings till twelve thirty. I was allowed a special train ticket for two and sixpence a week during my apprenticeship, the normal price was ten pence a day. I had six pence pocket money. It was there I met corrie, I sat next to her and we became lifelong friends. It was a very large factory, three stories high, ground floor was the cutting room, pressing room and packing room, second and third were all machinists, between two and three hundred. They were very high powered machines, I remember having my finger under once, the needle went right through my finger, one of the girls unscrewed the needle out of the machine and took me down to the tool room where a mechanic pulled it out with pliers. There was no canteen and no breaks morning or afternoon. We could have a cup of tea for 1d at dinner time, from what they called a kitchen, which was just a small room with a table and a large urn. We had to provide our own cup and sit at your machine to eat your lunch. At the end of the six months Carrie and I made the grade, you had to have speed and stitch perfectly, so we went piecework. To start off with they put us on overalls, ten pence a dozen. It was slave labour.

Five nights a week Ede would come home with me for tea and we would call at Elijahs for a two penny fish and a penny worth of chips, they were beautiful. It saved Mom having to cook and enabled Ede to see Fred, as she had to be home by eight thirty to serve in the pub her Dad kept. You may have wondered why I haven't mentioned my brother Stan, but he was the quiet one, his only interest was football. Stan and my Dad left the brickyard at the Hayes and went to work in the brickyard in Thorns Road, my Dad worked nights as night watchman so I didn't see much of him, as he was in bed all day and at work all night. Uncle Noah's lady friend passed away and Uncle Noah was taken ill and had to go to Knightwick Sanatorium on Ankerdine Hill. I remember Fred taking me in the lorry to visit him. He improved and allowed to come home again.

Meanwhile I had made friends with some girls who attended the congregational Church Sunday School Bible class and they got me to join them. I also joined their Girl Guide group and was made patrol leader. So many activities went on, they put on operettas, I was always in the chorus, the biggest show was put on at the Town Hall Stourbridge. It was too early to go home after our various practices, I had to be home by ten pm, so we would walk up and down the High Street, all teenagers congregated on the High streets, they were known as the monkey runs, shops kept open all hours, so they were well lit. It was on a Saturday night, I saw Stan for the first time, he stood in a shop doorway, and as we passed he offered me some chocolate which I refused and carried on, from then on I saw him often in Lye and eventually we got on speaking terms. Then one night he asked me to go to the pictures with him, so I thought why not, on 6d a week pocket money I couldn't afford to go mid week so I arranged to meet him by the library, the following night. He was there waiting for me and we stood chatting for a few minutes, looking across the road, there was my mother, and the look on her face. I knew I was in trouble, I told Stan to go as she came over to me. She asked me if I was with that lad and I said yes, and where were you thinking of going, so I told her in the Temp (cinema). Well, she said you can forget that you're too young and you are coming home with me. I was fifteen and Stan eighteen, I had been at work for twelve months but I felt like a little school kid. However going back down Lye who should we meet but my friends from the Congs and I told Mom I would stay with them, but I met Stan later on and he took me home. At the end of August he told me he had packed in his job and was going hop picking with his Aunty Lily, to, of all places, Leigh Court. This set my mind working. So I asked Mom if I could go to Mrs Dimmock for a week's holiday and she agreed, providing Mrs Dimmock was agreeable too. I was quaking in my shoes when I went in the office at work and asked for a week off, but they were quite nice with me, so I had my holiday. Stan had the shock of his life when he came out of their hut and saw me under the shanty, for he knew nothing of my plans and Mom never found out.

I still went to the "Congs" and had a special friend May Chance, and May and I decided to have our photograph taken at Hals in Stourbridge, I had six, kept two and gave the others to friends. I came home from work one night and Mom was all excited, we have a visitor, Bella Everson (she was later Mayoress of Stourbridge) had called to say I had been chosen as an attendant to the Carnival Queen, and would I go to her home for a dress fitting. I didn't want to go as I knew nothing at all about it. Another girl from our Sunday School had been chosen too and although I never found out, I think it must have been our Superintendent that sent our photographs to Sir Cedric Hardwick (the actor) to be judged. So I was on the 1930 carnival at Lye, I was sixteen years old.

Life carried on and I continued to see Stan despite all opposition. My brother Stan was going with a girl from Stourbridge, but she worked in a fish and chip shop and didn't finish until 11pm at night, so during the week I had Fred and Stan trying to track me down, I was always in trouble. My Uncle Noah was ill again and had to stay in bed and one night, I went upstairs to have a chat with him before going to meet Stan, and I found him hanging over the bed, dead. I ran downstairs to Mom, terrified, and when I met Stan that night I sobbed my heart out. I loved my Uncle Noah, the only one I could confide in and he never split on me. That was the first tragedy in my life. Fred married Ede and went to keep a pawn shop in Upper High Street, Lye, but life still wasn't easy for me. Every Sunday morning I had to clean Gran's room. The floor was all red quarries, just one podge rug on the hearth, which I had to take outside and give a good shake, clean the black leaded grate, and with a bucket of hot soapy water and floor cloth, I had to get down on my knees and wash all the tiles, and it was a big room. I hated doing it but it helped Mom as she had so much to do.

In Orchard Lane there was a bar across the road to stop vehicles going past the school, and one night Stan and I stood by this bar talking, and he said he wished he had a book to read, I said I had some he could borrow, so I went home to fetch them. Mom wanted to know where I was taking them, so I said I was lending them to a friend. I had just given them to Stan, looking up the road, there was Mother, waving an umbrella and it wasn't raining. I told Stan to go and realising she couldn't catch up with him, she walked me back home. She never said a word, but when we got back home she beat me unmercifully, my Dad who had come back for his supper, had to pull her away from me. I cried my eyes out on the stairs, I was innocent of doing anything wrong. So the next time I saw Stan I told him our friendship was finished, I couldn't take any more, but later fate was to step in. I told Mom and she was delighted, and I started to go dancing with Irene, an old friend. There was going to be a big dance at Stambermill Church Hall and I hadn't got a long dress to go in (they were the fashion in those days). Mom said don't worry I'll get you one. She went to Jeavons second hand shop and bought me one, and I wore it. The compere came over to me to start the dancing off, me in my second hand frock, and he was the son of the man who owned the brick yard where my Dad and brother worked.

A few weeks later when I got off the train from work, Doris, Stan's sister, was waiting for me. Stan was seriously ill with pneumonia and would I go home with her. I told her I would have to go home first and would come later. So I went home, had my tea and a wash, and explained to Mom about Stan. I didn't ask her permission, I said I was going and she never said a word. In those days people said that on the ninth day they passed a crisis they would either live or die, and this was the ninth day of Stan's illness, I sat on the bed holding his hand willing him to live. His Mom sat up all night with him. I went to his home the following night, not knowing whether he was alive or dead. I went to the back door, looking up I could see there was a light on in his bedroom. His Mom said she had had a terrible night with him, but he pulled through. He made a slow recovery and I visited every night. It was about six weeks later that he insisted on taking me home, on Lye Cross who should we meet but Mother, I waited for her reaction and to my surprise she couldn't have been nicer. She asked him if he was feeling better and said "my lad, you should not be out in this damp night air, Ellie, take him down home." I was flabberghasted, now my troubles were over.

When fully recovered he went back to work with his Dad in the spade and shovel works down Aston in Birmingham. He worked in the woodwork department, making the wooden handles, and although we both travelled to Birmingham we never met up as our timetables were different. I was doing all right at work, I would hand my pay packet to Mom and she would give me twho shillings and sixpence pocket money, out of which I had to buy my own stockings. One night Ede had a talk to her and told her she wasn't being fair to me, not giving me a chance to save any money, so Mom decided I should pay rent, which meant I gave her twelve and sixpence a week but had to buy my own clothes. Ede was now expecting and Fred asked Mom if it would be alright for me to have a fortnight off work, to look after the shop. So when Margaret was born I ran the pawn shop. I knew nothing at all about the running of it, but I soon learnt. One night Fred brought an old bike bac on his lorry, half the spokes were missing on the wheels, but I begged him to let me have it. So I took it home, never rode a bike but was determined to learn. I practiced down Engine Lane, the brakes weren't very good and being a man's bike, I had to grab the railway bridge to get off. I mastered it and later on I had a new bike from the Co-op. Stan had a bike and we did a lot of cycling together.

I was eighteen years old when we moved to number three Cross Walks, my granddad Taylor owned three cottages on Cross Walks, when one came empty he offered it to Dad, at first mom was reluctant to leave Gran as she was now confined to her bedroom and couldn't get down the stairs. On the day we moved Uncle Steve went mad, started breaking things up. He fetched the big water jug and bowl from downstairs and smashed it on the pavement, I tried to stop him and a piece of the platter fled up and cut my arm, so I ran as fast as I could to Lye Cross, a policeman was on duty, I explained to him what was happening and seeing the blood dripping from my arm he came with me. He restrained my Uncle and stayed until we were loaded up and away.

15

A few months after moving, Stan my brother got married to Vi at St john's Church at Stourbridge. I was bridesmaid and I made my own dress, I had the material from Lewis's in Birmingham. My Stan was invited and after the reception the four of us went to our Gran's, still in wedding attire to show her our dresses. Mom went every day to see to Gran's needs and during the Winter months Stan and I would go and spend an hour or more with her. No doors were ever locked in those days so we had no problem getting in, she would be there in bed, in total darkness, and we would light the candle on the chair at the side of the bed, and we would sit on the bed talking to her. What an existence! But she never complained, always pleasant, and a pleasure for us to visit her.

Fred moved from the pawn shop to Brockshop Hall in Dudley Road and it was there that Margaret took her first steps towards me. They didn't stay there long before moving to a farm in Netherend. My Gran passed away, she was eighty six years old. I was now twenty and I had to ask Mom if we could get engaged, she consented, and Stan gave me £5 to buy the ring. It was a lot of money in those days, more than Stan earned in a week. Mother went with me to Morris's to choose it. It was November but I didn't wear it until Christmas Day. She said I could get married when I was twenty one providing we found somewhere to live, so I started buying things for my bottom drawer when I had spare cash. We would go by train 2d return to Cradley market, a very big outdoor market which kept open till 9pm. It was there we met Stan and Nancy (Janice's Mom and Dad) and we became lifelong friends. We made up a foursome and went out together, every weekend we tried to do something different. One Saturday night we hired a rowing boat on the canal at Halesowen, neither of us had been in a boat before. The men took turns to row and Nancy and I to steer , laugh? We went from one side of the canal to the other, and at one point we got stuck in the reeds. We managed to get to the Black horse pub, where we got out for a drink. We got back safe, but never went again.

Now back to Fawcetts. One afternoon the R101 airship passed over Birmingham, it passed right in front of our factory, blocking out all the windows, scared us all, couldn't think what it was. Later on it went up in flames over France. I had progressed well and any samples that came up the foreman would pass on to me and I was paid 3d extra, but my days were numbered there. Stuart Golfar were opening a sewing factory in Stourbridge and I applied for a job there. I left Birmingham, it was great working near home, I went on my bike and went home for my dinner every day. We were now looking for a house, with marriage in mind, and Stan told me of a new housing estate being built in Quinton, two show houses were built and furnished, so we went to see them. They were lovely, so we decided we would go in for one, we picked out the plot and paid the deposit. When I told Mother, she went mad, it was too far away, what if Stan was ill and couldn't pay the mortgage, she went on and on, she worried me so much we cancelled it. We were back to square one, Frede and Ede were on the move again, they left the farm and went to keep the wollescote stores in Belmont.

Ede was pregnant again and Fred asked me to have time off again to take charge of the shop when the baby was born. I kney it left him in a quandary but I had to turn him down and make him realise I was no longer at his beck and call.

I was now twenty two years old, I heard of a house empty in Atwood Street, I knew the landlord well and coming down the street one Saturday morning I met him, stopped him and asked if I had any chance of having it. He said "Nellie, if you want it, it's yours". I went home and told Mom. She was all excited and said we must go to Stambermill Church and put the Banns in that afternoon, as I would have to start paying rent. I said I couldn't do that until I had talked it over with Stan, so she said go and meet him from work. He always went to work on his bike Saturday mornings and I knew he would be on the Hayes around 1pm. So I met him, talked things over and he told me to carry on with the arrangements. He went home, had his dinner and went to bed, never said a word to his mother. When he got up at teatime, there was a real confloption. A man had called from the Eagle

House in Stourbridge (a large furniture shop) asking if her son would give them the order for his furniture. Now they had not long moved into a new house, taken out a mortgage and were relying on Stan's wages to help pay for it, and was dead against us getting married, but our plans went ahead.

The landlord had the house decorated all through, Sim Taylor had a furniture shop right opposite, so Mom and I went to see him and he told me to have everything I wanted. I told him I couldn't afford to do that, but he said that's alright, pay down what you can and the rest later, so as each room was finished his son laid the lino and carried the furniture in, so we had a house fully furnished to move into. He even gave me a basket chair, half a tea set and a doormat. He was a good old soul and helped a lot of people in Lye. I made my own dress, also Margaret's and Bill's outfit (he was Stan's younger brother). Both were five years old so we married at Stambermill Church November 14th 1936. I continued to work and Mom was good to me, she did my washing and would bring it back ironed. On Saturday afternoons we would go to Cradley market, everything was cheaper there, and she learnt me the different joints of beef, I always came back with a Sunday roast for one and eight pence. Stan and mom got on fine and whatever she bought Fred and Stan for Christmas, my Stan had the same. I think my mother in law really hated me for going against her wishes, the first Christmas card we sent was pushed back under the door, and she would ignore me if she saw me in the High Street. It worried me at first, but Stan said not to let her upset me, she would relent given time, but it took a heck of a long time.

Carrie, my friend from Birmingham came to my wedding and we corresponded by letter frequently, and we still went out with Stan and Nance Saturday nights, sometimes to the last house in the Central picture house in Stourbridge. There was always a long queue to get in, there was a little cook shop in New Street where they did hot meat sandwiches and we would call at the Labour in Vain pub to wash them down, or go to Cradley Heath and call in Lomy Town for fish and chips and back home on the train, just simple things but we enjoyed our nights out together.

It was 1937, May 12th, the coronation of King George VI and Queen Elizabeth (Queen Mother) and we found out there was an excursion running to London on the 13th, so the four of us decided to go. It was a wonderful sight, everything was just as it had been the day before. We went to Westminster Abbey where they were crowned, the flower arrangements were out of this world. Every street was decorated with flowers, flags and streamers. There was a big shop, I can't remember if it was Selfridges or Harrods, but it had silk draped on the outside of every window, and window boxes full of exotic flowers beneath, we walked the length of the Mall to Buckingham Palace, picnicked in a park and made our way back to the station, tired and weary but we had a great day.

I have over run my story, I'm back to Fred and Ede again, not able to find anybody to run the shop, they had to move out, and having nowhere to go, they moved in with Mom. I married and left on the Saturday and Mary was born the next Saturday at 3 Cross Walks. As soon as Ede was over her confinement, they went to live with Uncle Steve in Engine Lane. They were not there long, Uncle Steve passed away, the house not being in their name, they had to move on, this time to the White Horse pub in Cradley. They didn't stay there long before moving to Brook Street Lye and finally to Balds Lane, which they made their permanent home and started his potato business.

A few weeks after we were married Stan had a spate of boils on the back of his neck and he was in agony. From the work they sent him to the general hospital, where they told him he must change his job, the sawdust was the cause, clogging all the pores. So he left Birmingham and got a job at the Co-op factory in Dudley, making safes and steel office furniture. A special works bus ran from Lye Cross at 7.45 and brought them home, so there was no transport problems. Working in Birmingham he had to get up at 5.30am to catch the 6.15 train six mornings a week, so he bettered himself all ways.

1937. During that year I remember treating my Mom to a day's outing. I booked a coach trip to Rhyl, she had never been on a coach, I don't think she had been any further than Cradley Heath on a train and had never seen the sea. It was a lovely Summer's day and how she enjoyed it. We did another trip to Brighton with Stan and Nance, and that was our lot, we couldn't afford a week's holiday. Vi, my brother Stan's wife gave birth to a son Stanley on November 1st, and by the end of December I had paid off all my debts.

1938. I became pregnant and I worked up until the August holidays. One day the woman who lived at No 3 The Dock came to see me and asked if I would change houses with her. She wanted to be near her father and sister and as we both had the same landlord there was no problem there, so we moved during the August holidays while Stan was at home. I stayed to see that everything was loaded up and when I went to No 3 The Dock who should be in the living room, my mother in law. It had taken nearly two years to bury the hatchet, and I know why. She knew I was pregnant, and didn't intend moving out on her first grandchild. He was born on December 8th 1938, weighed 9.5 pounds at birth and was Christened six weeks later, Colin Stanley, at the congregational Church, Lye. The service was early on the Sunday morning, Mom came with us and Fred Walton and his wife were God parents. They came back for a drink then went home. Stan took Colin in his pram to visit his Mom. Every Saturday afternoon, Edith, Stan's sister would come and take Colin out and Mom and I would go and do our weekend shopping. He was a very good baby, never had to get up in the night, and good during the day. But come tea time when I had to cook our main meal, he would bawl his head off, just as if he knew he wasn't going to get any attention from me. Often I would take him up to Mom's, with his dummy and a jar of Virol, she would welcome him with open arms. I would fetch him back as soon as I had finished cooking. Mom lived just two minutes walk away.

1939. September 3rd War was declared, Colin was just 9 months old. I listened to every news bulletin on the radio wondering what was going to happen. All young men were called up for the forces and the women who had no young children had to go to work in the ammunition factories. The Co-op changed over to war work so Stan was exempt. We had to have black out blinds for all our windows, no lights had to be showing, and all street lights were turned off. They started putting air raid shelters in back yards, making sure everybody had somewhere to go, should there be a raid. We didn;t have one as we had a large arched cellar, where they said we would be quite safe, Near our home was the Church Hall, this was taken over by the fire service and in the yard they erected the siren, to alert everybody in Lye. It was only a few yards away from our bedroom window. I'll never forget the first night it sounded, I was all of a shake, couldn't get dressed quick enough, rolled Colin in a shawl and fled down the two flights of steps into the cellar. We were to have many nights down there, but none as nerve wracking as the first time. Ours was a most peculiar house, two stories high at the front and three at the back. We had a front, side and back door, entering by the side door, to the right was the front room which was on ground level. To the left was the living room, which was on the second floor, quite a pleasant outlook and leading off the living room were the nine steps leading into the coal cellar. The coal was tipped through a grating under the front window and passing through another small archway you were in what I called the under kitchen. There was a sink, gas boiler, toilet, washing machine, window and door leading to the back yard, and electric lights. We had a sink unit in the living room so I didn't have to go down the cellar for water. My store was on the top of the cellar head. It was arranged for an elderly couple, Mr and Mrs Brown, who kept the sweet shop at the bottom of Love Lane, and Lizzie who lived at the back of the shop next door, to come to our cellar when the siren sounded. I felt sorry for Lizzie, her husband had been called up and she had a child the same age as Colin. She would come dashing over with Royston in his pram, all of a shake. The back door was never locked and we could push the pram through into the coal cellar. We had a big old armchair and chairs, where they came from I don't know, everybody helped each other out, Stan would make us hot drinks, and with a toilet handy, we were a few of the lucky ones.

We would sit listening to the drone of the German planes overhead, not knowing where they would drop their load, but Birmingham was their target, and as the bombs dropped the ground would shake under us, and so the months passed by. Carrie was married and had a little girl Maureen, Harry, her husband, had been called up and was in the Navy on a minesweeper, she wrote and told me they were in the shelter every night, so I invited her over. She came two weekends and luckily we had no alerts. Stan slept downstairs on the couch, Corrie, Maureen and I were in a bed. She was later evacuated to Tibshelf in Derbyshire, we still corresponded. We were issued with ration books, everything was in short supply, always queues. I always went to the Co-op on a Friday night for our rations, having three books I would have six ounces of butter; six ounces of margarine; six ounces of lard; one packet of tea; six ounces of cheese and if I was lucky, a tin of Nestles condensed milk, a tin of custard powder, and anything off rations. I wrapped everything in to a large piece of brown paper and tied it up with string. I would go to Marsh and Baxters, a well noted pork butchers shop in Lye, where, when available, you could buy what they termed as offal, sometimes a bit of liver, pigs tails, chitterlings and pork bones. I would boil the bones and when cold skim off the fat, which I used to make some pastry, scraped all the meat off the bones, fry an onion, mix with the meat and the pastry on top, it made a meal. Mother would be out every morning to see what was going, she would queue for sweets or buns for the grandchildren. During the Winter months Stan never saw daylight, it would be dark when he left in the morning, all the windows were blacked out, and dark when he got home at night. Twice a week he had to do fire watching at a wood factory all night as well. Tom, Stan's younger brother had met Marj and he brought her to our house often. It was coming up to Christmas, there were no toys in the shops, so Stan decided to make a train in sheet metal for Colin, and a set of dominoes. After I had got Colin off to bed at night, Tom and Marj, and Harry, another brother would come, and sit filing the metal from the spikes at the wheels for this train, and Marj and I had the job of painting the white spots and lines on the dominoes. He also made the two weighing scales for Margaret and Mary. He assembled the train at work, it was about eighteen inches long, with a coal tender and one wagon at the back. It was a replica of a steam train. Was Colin proud of that train, I can remember Christmas morning, we tied some string to the front and he pulled it up the street to show his Granny Taylor, and being sheet metal it made such a clatter.

Colin started school in the January following his third birthday, his first day over, I asked him if he enjoyed it, his reply was, "it was alright but I don't think I'll go tomorrow!" So the months passed, nothing improved. There were no gas fires or electric, everybody depended upon coal. I had always dealt with the Co-op coalman, and always kept a good supply, but it had dwindled and not knowing when I would get the next lot, I would go and queue at Sammy Cramptons, a coal merchant who lived opposite the village church, of course his regular customers would be served first, any left you would be allowed half a hundredweight, half of it would be in bags, or half a hundredweight of coke. He would tip it into a barrow, you had to wheel it home and return the barrow, it was hard going.

Tom was the first to be called up in their family, it broke his mother's heart as he was her favourite son. Jack and Bill followed later. He joined the Reconnaissance Corp. And Marj joined the ATS.

One afternoon I answered a knock on our front door, outside two men were unloading a piano, I told them they had come to the wrong house, they said no, a Mrs Sidaway had given them my address, so the piano was bought into my front room. It was old but had been kept in beautiful condition. Stan was highly delighted, they had always had a piano at home and he could play. How or where it came from we never knew, mother-in-law said she had had it given to her. It was a bit hard to swallow but we let it pass. Tom could play the piano too. He was stationed in Colchester, and when he came on leave he would travel at night, get the first early morning train from Birmingham, call at our house first, shout through the letter box "Come on Nell, I'm here!" Letting him in he would go straight to the piano and start playing "In the mood". He was a darling, we knew there would be no peace until he went back.

Colin was now about four years old, it was Thursday and he had been playing in the Dock with a gang of children. When he came in his face was flushed and his hair soaked in sweat, I had a terrible night with him. So before going to work Stan went to Mom's and asked her to go to the doctors and ask him to call. After examining him, he said he would like him to go to Hayley Green hospital, as he thought he had diphtheria. I was not allowed to go with him but the following day being Saturday was the normal visiting day, so I thought we wouldn't have long to wait. So Stan and I went, full of hope, we had to walk as there was no transport. It was an isolation hospital and visitors had to stand outside and look in through the windows. But we couldn't find Colin, a nurse came outside, I explained who we were and she said Matron wished to speak to us in her office. She said she was very sorry to give us the sad news but there's very little hope for him, she shook her head. Then she said had he been inoculated he would have stood a chance, so I said he had been three months ago. The doctor never asked me that when he took particulars I pleaded with her to let me see him, I promised not to break down so she relented. We had to put on white coats and masks, he knew me and understood what I said to him, but he was so ill. We had to leave a phone number in case we were needed during the night, so I gave them Fred's number as he was the only one I knew who had a phone. I called at Mom's on the way home and the floodgates opened. We had a house full of people that night, even the Salvation Army out selling their War Cries heard the news, came to our house and prayed for him. I will never forget that night. We went again on the Sunday, there was a little improvement. With their permission I was allowed to take Mom to see him. She asked him what he would like her to bring him, his reply, one of Taylor's custards.

On the way home she said "Now what am I going to do, even if I can get one I couldn't just take it into that hospital." So instead of going to the shop she went to the bakery, asked to see Mr Taylor and came away with a dozen. She was so pleased, couldn't get to the hospital quick enough the next day. We were allowed to visit any time the first week, then as he improved, it was just Saturday afternoons and no one allowed in. The Salvation Army captain Mr Marham, would visit him during the week, entertain him with his puppet and report back to me. He did wonderful work during those war years. Colin was in hospital for eight weeks, I had to push him around in his old pushchair as he was too weak to walk. When he came home, he slowly recovered and I took him hop picking. Stan said he could look after himself during the week and he would come down on the train Saturday afternoons and go back Sunday nights. I took Colin's pushchair, it was very useful, I would push him to the hop fields and it enabled us to go to the Bear public house on a Saturday night, which was almost two miles away. As I said before, they had built new huts and one was used as a shop, and as we were classed as farm workers we were allowed extra rations, we could buy as much cheese as we wished.

Stan always went home with a pound of cheese, some bacon and butter to see him through the week. We were there four weeks and all the fresh air did Colin the world of good. The next year Colin was sent to the open air school at Malvern for three months and parents were only allowed one visit during that time. But his Uncle Tom came home on leave, so we tried to wangle another visit, and Tom in his uniform, they allowed us in.

We went hop picking again in September, it was a break for me, and the iar suited Col and we both loved it. Back home again and the war dragged on, next door lived three teenage girls, their mother died when they were young, then their Nan died at the start of the war. They were terrified when the siren started so they asked Stan if they could bring one of their beds into our cellar, he couldn't refuse and they slept down there until nearly the end of the war. They opened a

British restaurant at the bottom of Talbot Street and I would take Colin most days. He didn't like the dinners but he liked the puddings, so I would buy him one and give him mine, at least he had something warm to go back to school on.

Stan's Dad became very ill and had to go to hospital, I was going hop picking, so we took colin up to Corbetts hospital to see his Granddad, children weren't allowed in. His bed was by a window, so we lifted him up so he was able to see and talk to his Granddad. A week later he passed away. Stan came down to Leigh Court and we went back with him for the funeral. Col and I returned to the country the next day, as we had left our belongings there and we stayed to the end of the season.

We joined the Liberal Club and spent many happy hours there. We made friends with Marj's Mom and Dad, who were also members, and their friends Mr and Mrs Hudson, she was Canadian and he came from London, a very jolly couple. They had a son and daughter Ray and Lillian, Lillian's young man was in the RAF, very tall and very smart in his uniform. Occasionally Marj, Tom and Ray would be on leave together and we would have a good get together. There was a large snooker room with two full size snooker tables, and seats all around, this is where we would congregate. Stan loved a game of snooker or billiards and children were allowed in. We started a social cub, they let us use an upstairs room, just one night a week. Harry Matten, who ran a concert party would come along with his pianist and entertain us, we would have competitions, and out of the small subs we had to pay they bought small prizes. One night they announced there was a prize for the person with the dirtiest shoes, everybody was looking at their shoes when in walks Colin, he walked away with the prize. It was a plastic holder with black and brown shoe polish, two brushes and a duster. I still have the holder.

Moving on, it was Christmas time, Tom and Marj came on embarkation leave, tom was being sent to Egypt and Marj to Germany, and they decided to get married, with so little time it was hectic. She had a married sister that lived in a large flat over Adam's butchers shop opposite the Clifton which is now Lye Market and it was decided the reception would be held there. I remember going round to all my friends asking if they could spare a spoonful of tea, sugar, a jelly, food was still on rations. She only had to buy her bouquet, she borrowed a white wedding dress, veil, head dress and sandals. And so they were married in Church, Marj in white and Tom in uniform. The reception was held at Joyce's (Marj's sister) they had borrowed trestle tables and chairs from the liberal club also their piano, and how they got it up the stairs I'll never know. Mr Cheetham the Clifton manager came over after the cinema closed, he was a brilliant pianist and the party went on and on, it was 4am when we went home.

Tom and Marj stayed with her sister and two days later they travelled down to Dover, not knowing when they would see each other again. He asked me to write to him every week, we corresponded regularly and he sent me numerous snaps, and photographs to reassure us he was safe and well. The years rolled on and gradually we were coming back to a normal way of life, no more nights in the cellar, but food was still in short supply. We decided to go on holiday, so we went to Morecambe by train and stayed in a small cottage on the sea front. It's now an ice cream parlour. As soon as we arrived we made friends with a couple who were staying there, she was very outgoing and said she had been a ballet dancer in her younger days. Now Colin had started piano lessons and taken his music with him, there was a piano in the room and he told her he could play. "Oh" she said "come along sweetie pie, you play and I'll dance" so as he played Bertie's Birthday she pirouetted around the room. It broke the ice with everyone and we had a smashing holiday, we went again the next year. Still went hop picking during September.

The British Restaurant closed down and Stuart Golfars opened a sewing factory there, as it was so near home I started work there. They had a small canteen and during the morning break we had a round of toast and a cup of tea for 2d. The cook made little cakes for our afternoon break. I kept mine for Colin, he was allowed to come into the factory, eat his cake and wait for me to finish work at 4.30. But my easy life was to come to an end, my Mother became ill and we couldn't make out what was the matter with her. I took her to see the doctor, he examined her and gave her medicine that made her worse. We were all getting worried and not telling anyone I decided to find out. I saw her doctor, and he handed me her notes, told me to read what he had written down when he examined her, cancer of the liver. He also told me she could live for another three months, at the most six months, I was shattered. It was a Friday night and I went back to Mom's, knowing my brother Stan would be there, as he visited mom every Friday night. Ede, Fred's wife, was there too. Not saying anything in front of them I waited for Ede to go, and making an excuse, I had forgotten to tell her something, I ran after Ede, and told her the sad news. She was terribly upset, she regarded my Mom as her own mother, as her own Mother passed away when she was a child. So I went back to Mom's doing my best to put on a brave face and waited for Stan to leave. Walking down the street I broke the news to him. We were all devastated, talking things over with Stan, I decided to pack in my job, so I was free to look after Mom. Now next door but one lived a fellow and after his Mother passed on and having no other relationship, Mother took pity on him and had done his washing, cooking him a dinner on weekdays. She asked me to carry on, so I had Mom and Dad, Vernie and Colin to cook for. I would have my main meal with Stan at tea time. Thank goodness there were shops near, no need to go down into Lye. She gradually got worse, in terrible pain, and had to stay in bed. A fortnight before Christmas the doctor sent her to Corbett's Hospital, and she seemed to improve. Ede and I went to visit her two days before Christmas Day and she begged us to take her home, Ede pleaded with her, saying she would be better looked after there. I knew Ede was thinking of me too, but she started to cry, I had never seen my Mother cry, it was too much for me, so I promised she would go home the next day. It was Christmas Eve, I took all her clothes, helped her to get dressed and she walked out of that hospital, but I had to get her to bed when we got home. Christmas Day, I was cooking a chicken and a large joint of pork, so I dished up a dinner with some chicken for Mom, Dad carried it up, leaving the pork to carry on cooking while I was away. I stayed while she ate her dinner and when I got home Stan had laid the table in the front room, we were going to dine in style. Only to find when I opened the oven door, all the rind on the pork was burnt black. Stan said never mind Nell, I'll cut off all the burnt. After tea all Stan's family came to our house as usual, but I was in no mood for entertaining and went up to Mom's. Stan's mother came with me.

The days dragged on and Mom was confined to bed. I really needed help so I went to see nurse Dunn, she was a retired lady and knew Mom well, and agreed to come every day. We knew her end was near and I would stay with her till midnight. One night she asked me to stay until she had said her prayer, and she said the first verse of Abide with me. I knew then that she knew too, it was heartbreaking. Even now I get a lump in my throat whenever I hear that hymn. She passed away in the early hours of Jan 20th 1949, not peacefully, in agony. Her son Stan, Fred, Dad, the nurse and myself were with her.

During 1948 Tom and Marj came home and stayed with Marj's sister Joyce. Now Joyce and Wilf were going to Bournemouth on holiday, so Tom and Marj went with them. While there they decided to stay . Tom got a job in a grocer's shop and Marj at Harvey Nicholls. They got furnished rooms, never to return to the midlands to live again. After all the trauma I was not well and had lost a lot of weight, and Marj invited me down there for a break. Stan had no objection and would look after Colin, so I went for a fortnight. Coming back I still had Dad and Vernie to look after, which meant I was running three homes. I could have stopped looking after Vern, but the money he paid me helped me out.

Colin had passed for the Grammar School having had so much time off school owing to illness it was a surprise to us, but we were very pleased. He was also doing well with his piano lessons. Carrie, my friend in Birmingham, had a nice piano her parents had bought new, haing passed on she inherited it. She now had three children and would never be able to afford to have them taught to play it. Harry needed a new suit, so she said if we would pay for a suit we could have it. So a deal was made, our paino went to a pub in Lye. Fred Walton fetched it in his lorry and Harry had his suit.

The three girls next door all married and left and the landlord begged us to buy, he offered us the two houses for £500, but we hadn't got that much money, so we missed out on that bargain. With Colin's education in mind we didn't want to get into any debts, our rent was only eight shillings a week. Mr and Mrs Homer bought the property and came to live next door.

Stan left the Co-op and went to work for Tooby and Sons in Stourbridge, painting and decorating. He had never done that kind of work but was willing to learn, and stayed there for a number of years. I remember the first car he bought, his younger brother Bill, who had learned to drive in the army was going to teach him to drive. It was an old thing with blown up seats, I told him he would never get me to go out in it, so they took it to a garage and part exchanged it for a Morris. He passed his test first time in it.

Colin did well in his O Levels, but didn't want to carry on at school, his headmaster got him an interview with a firm in Birmingham, so he started work in the offices of Crittalls in heating and air conditioning. He also had to attend Dudley Technical College once or twice a week, plus evening classes. They were long days for him, his Dad would go in all weathers to pick him up in Dudley to save him hanging around for buses.

I must include our day out with Stan's brother Jack and Josie, it was Easter and we decided to go to Southport on Bank holiday Monday. Jack said we would go in his car, as it had been checked over at a garage and more reliable than ours. Stan let Bill and Bett, "his girlfriend" and Colin have our car for the day. So we all set off, we had a good day and picnicked in the sand dunes. On returning home we met up with all the traffic from Blackpool and as it got dark we had no lights and eventually came to a full stop. Stan, Josie and I got out and pushed the car until the engine started, this went on for mile after mile. It was 10pm when we pulled into a garage, they said it would take three hours to charge the battery, so Jack decided to carry on. We went on for a few more miles but at the bottom of a step hill it finally stopped. At the top of the hill we had passed a garage but it was closed so there was no alternative, we would have to spend the night in the car. It was bitterly cold, no water to make a hot drink and no way we could get in touch with Colin to let him know we were safe. As dawn broke I saw a farmhouse, I waited until I saw smoke coming out of the chimney and taking the kettle, off I went up the lane. As I entered the farmyard an old lady came out of the house, she had a mop cap on her head and a piece of sacking round her waist, really queer. I asked if I could have a kettle of water, she pointed to a pump and told me to help myself and away she went. Tea had never tasted so good, it was the first we had had since leaving Southport the previous afternoon. The men set off to see if they could get help from the garage at the top of the hill. They returned with a mechanic, he brought another battery and fitted a new pump. We were away in no time at all, arriving home at 9am. Colin had gone to work so I rang the office to let him know all was well. What a night that was.

So the years went by, as Dad grew older the more trouble he became. I had to carry all his meals up to him, although we lived a short distance away, I had to climb a steep hill. He had four sisters who lived quite near, but not one came to see him. Mom had been gone eight years when one Friday night I took him his tea as usual and found him sitting on the couch trying to light his pipe, matches and tobacco all over the floor. When I spoke to him his voice was slurred and I knew something was wrong. I took his matches off him and told him I would light his pipe when I came back. I went straight for his doctor, called at home and Stan came with me. The doctor confirmed he had had a seizure and must not be left alone, and they got him into bed. I stayed with him until midnight when Stan relieved me, same again on Saturday. I couldn't get him to eat or drink, Sunday morning Stan went for nurse Bishop, she tried to give him a drink but it just trickled out of his mouth. So we had another day and night vigil, we were both shattered and when the doctor called on the Monday morning he said he would do his best to get him away, and that night he was admitted to All Saints hospital in Bromsgrove. He lived another fifteen months, we visited every Sunday afternoon. He passed away July 1959 aged 82 years.

Vernie had been rehoused into a council flat and I was now free of all obligation. Tom and Marj invited me down for a holiday, they had left Bournemouth and gone to keep a newsagents in Hamworthy, near Poole. They now had two children, Judith who was three years old and Peter, who was a baby. It was a quaint little place, every morning I took the children to Hamworthy beach, Peter in the pram and Judith trotting along at the side. Later on Tom bought the shop and we had many holidays with them. Returning I started work at Golfar's sewing factory, Stan left Tooby's and started working on his own, painting and decorating. We made friends with a couple who lived on the other side of the road, a Mr and Mrs Marshall, they had bought a cottage down Martley and he asked if Stan would be interested in decorating it. He took us down to see it one Saturday night, it was very old and isolated, with a stream running down a spinney, and a little wooden bridge over the stream leading to a large paddock. Stan took on the work and took two young lads to help him out. Marshall was going down one afternoon and Stan asked him if he could take me with him. It was a hot summer's day and I asked if they would like me to make them a cup of tea before starting back. I found the kettle but there was no tap over the sink, Marshall said there was a well over in the paddock. I found it, it had been bricked over, with a wooden door at the front. As the door was at ground level I had to get down on my hands and knees. Opening the door I looked in, it was full of frogs. I swirled the kettle round and managed to fill it. I went back and made the pot of tea. Waiting until they had drunk it, I asked if they had enjoyed it, they thanked me and said it was very nice. I said you have had tea made with frog water, as the well is full of frogs. The one young lad dashed outside heaving his heart out. Needless to say I didn;t have any, I hate frogs, but they didn't suffer any after effects.

Stan dealt with Manders in Stourbridge for all his paint and wallpaper, and I had just arrived home from work one afternoon when there was a knock on the front door and in front of the window was a Manders van. Opening the door there were two men, who said they were delivering the wallpaper. Thinking nothing of it I told them to bring it in, thinking it would just be a couple of boxes. After six boxes I said "hang on, how many more?" they said it was a van load. Stan had only bought all Manders discontinued stock and never told me. They stacked them on top of the piano, settee, armchairs and every bit of floor space. When Stan came home I gave him a piece of my mind, but he said "don't worry Nell we'll get rid of it, when you go to work tomorrow, tell all your friends we have wallpaper at one shilling and sixpence a roll." The news soon got round and we barely had time to our tea before people were knocking on the door. We got rid of it and had a holiday in Blackpool out of the profit.

I can't remember what year it was but we were members of the Liberal club and there was an election coming up. I went to the meetings, helping to address envelopes but they had a problem, they needed a committee room. So I volunteered with the landlord's permission, they could have the use of our front room. Mr Homer was a strong Liberal and gave me consent. They kept us supplied with sandwiches from the club and I supplied the drinks. After tea, members who had cars came along and I went with them, collecting people who had difficulty getting to a polling station. We didn't win the election but we had a great day and celebrated at the club afterwards.

We had made friends with a couple, Mollie and Howard, he was a self employed builder, and we went out with them most weekends in their

Morris Oxford car. Stan had bought his first new car, a little A35 van, which was more suitable for his work than a car. We decided to go on holiday together, but we wanted a holiday with a difference, so we planned to take the two cars abroad and try and get to Spain. Stan got in touch with the RAC and they sent us maps and itineraries, and we booked the ferry. We started off for Dover on the Friday lunchtime, Howard had his two sons with them, Barry who was 14 years and Royston 17. There were no motorways and we went all the way round to avoid going through London. It was getting dark and pouring with rain so we booked in to a hotel in Reigate for the night, reaching the docks next morning. We had a lovely crossing and landed in Calais bang on lunchtime. We were able to take the lead, I remember Stan telling me not to speak to him for the next half hour, what with driving on the opposite side of the road, the streets were all cobbles and bikes were coming from all directions. As we left the town there were rows of small houses, riddled with bullet holes from the war. We got as far as Abbeville and booked into a small hotel, terrible place, but it had a court yard with large iron gates, we drove in and the gates were locked, so at least the cars were safe.

Next morning we were away early, after about an hour we stopped and cooked breakfast on the side of the road. We had everything in our van for our use, a bottle of gas, water carrier and a double burner. Moving on we came to Rouen, all traffic was being moved to the side of the road. De Gaulle was going to church. Our van overheated, we would have to wait until it had cooled down. The gendarmes started to move the traffic on, one came over to us, he made Howard understand he would have to move on, but we could stay. Howard was worried, Stan told him to carry on until he came to a car park and we would find him later. Royston, their eldest son, stayed behind with us. We found them and hit the trail again and stayed overnight in a motel near Vierzon. Travelled all day Monday and got as far as Toulouse, staying overnight in a hotel. Next morning Howard said he'd had enough, he thought we ought to turn back. Stan said if that's how you feel start back now, "but if it takes me the rest of my holiday I'm going to Spain". So he said in that case he "would have to follow you because I'd never find my way back." We reached the frontier on top of the Pyrenees early Tuesday afternoon and drove down to the Costa Brava. We pulled in at a little town called Blanes, parked on the sea front and went into a bar for a drink. The language was a problem, but after a bit of miming, the waiter understood what we were looking for. He gave us the name of several hotels, walking down the front we came to the San Francisco, outside was a board with a menu in English on it, so we booked in, bed and breakfast and evening meal, all for twenty two shillings a day. We had our own bathroom and breakfast was served under the trees on the sea front. It was a very old and undeveloped town and every morning little donkey drawn carts loaded with produce would come to a little open market place, there was a fish market there too.

Every night at 6pm we would go to the harbour and watch the fishermen unload their catch, some queer fish among them too. It would be sold on the market next day. Our cars were parked on the sea front right opposite our hotel and one morning we went to the cars before going out for the day, only to find our van had been broken into. They had broken the lock on the back door, we reported it to the manager in the hotel, he told us to make a list of all that had been stolen, he would sign it and claim off your insurance. He said if we reported it to the police we would not be allowed to leave Spain until the culprit was found. Stan tied the back door with string and Howard backed his car up against it. As we stood talking Barry got in their car and put the catch down in the door when he got out. Howard asked him for the keys, he had left them in the ignition, his Dad blew his top. We had two cars, one we couldn't lock and the other we couldn't open. Royston managed to find a piece of wire and prised the small vent at the side of the car and got the keys. There were no more mishaps, we had a wonderful holiday and came back quicker than we went, vowing that we would go again next year.

I had to relate all our adventures to the girls at work. Now Ernie's Premium Bond draw had started, and discussing it one day, I told them I was going to save £1 a week and at the end of the month I would buy a £5 bond, and if it didn't win anything it would pay for my holiday the next year, but only I got around to buying one. It was winter again, snow on the ground, one afternoon Stan arrived before me, so I asked him to fetch some fish and chips from Oldswinford. He was away so long, he said he thought he saw Bob Taylor's car on the forecourt of the garage in Hagley Road, Stourbridge and pulled in to have a chat. I was mistaken and stopped, talking to a salesman, and guess what Nell, I have traded the van in for a new Cortina Estate. I couldn't believe what I was hearing, he said it's true and it was being delivered the following Wednesday. Right, now where are the fish and chips, I asked. In his excitement he had forgotten what he had originally gone for and had to go back again. It was a lovely car, pale blue with a white flash along the sides and very useful for carrying all his gear to work.

Another incident I must record. The Liberal Club was closed on Sundays and we often went to the Hundred House, a little pub not many yards from where we lived. When we went in the landlord handed a large parcel to Stan, saying Charlie Lloyd had left it for him. Charlie worked in undertaking in Birmingham, couldn't think what it could be and we didn't open it until we got home. I nearly died, it was a miniature coffin, covered in purple baize with miniature brass handles and brass plate with Stan's name, saying "Rest in Peace". Stan put it on the sideboard, I couldn't touch it. Stan's mother called, I thought she would be upset, but no, she said "Oh, what a lovely thing, keep it, you would be able to put his ashes in it." The following Sunday morning, I couldn't stand seeing it any longer, so I unscrewed the brass handles and put it on the fire and went down the cellar to finish my washing. A short time after someone came to the back door, did I know my chimney was on fire? I dashed upstairs, threw a packet of salt on the fire which put it out. The smoke had blown away from the house and held all the traffic up on the High Street and filled the Hundred House pub. Charlie said he made it as a joke and was sorry it had upset me.

Colin no longer lived at home, he had been to college in London for nearly two years and coming back he couldn't settle down. He still worked for the Birmingham firm and bought himself an A40 van. He got himself a flat in Dudley for a time, then went to live on the canal on a boat. He came to visit us at least twice a week, I did all his washing and ironing and he knew where to come for a good meal. He was now 24 or 25 years old and free to do as he wished.

So back to us again and thinking about holidays we decided on Spain with Howard and family, but a month before we were due to go, Howard wasn't feeling well and didn't think he ought to make the journey. Meanwhile Stan had already booked our ferry, so we went on our own. We went via London to Dover where we stayed overnight and caught a very early crossing. We travelled well and arrived at a motel at Vierzon the first night, away early next morning and got as far as Montauban in the south of France, staying overnight at a motel. There was the main hotel where you could have a meal but the chalets were wooden cabins set amongst the trees, they had bathrooms and all mod cons, very quaint. We arrived at Blanes late Sunday afternoon, same hotel, they were so pleased to see us, after unpacking we went down into the bar. The boss came over to us and bought Stan a beerand got the bar tender to mix me a San Francisco cocktail, it was delicious. While standing at the bar, a fellow got talking to Stan in broken English, he and his wife were Dutch, he introduced himself and his wife, Jacques and Fie. She couldn't speak a word of English so it was impossible for me to hold a conversation with her. After a time Stan apologised, it was time for us to go in for our evening meal, so Jacques said perhaps we meet again tomorrow, they were staying at another hotel. After breakfast the next morning they were there waiting for us. They were a very nice couple and we went out with them most of our holiday.

I have overrun my tale, I forgot to mention we got lost in the Pyrenees, going through the frontier Stan took the wrong turning and for four hours we drove through the mountains, the only people we saw were some gypsies with a horse drawn cart. We had to keep going, because had we turned back we would have run out of petrol. I was scared, those mountains are so wild. We eventually came to an outpost, two soldiers stopped us with guns on their hips and searched our car. A lot of smuggling went on in those days, from Andorra. Satisfied we were tourists they waved us on, language was the problem, there were two roads and a signpost both pointing to Barcelona. I had a brainwave, I just said "Gerona" and pointed to which road we should take. We gradually drove into the foothills and passing through a small town I saw a sign GAZ. Stan pulled in and filled the tank. We made it to Gerona and Blanes was only half an hour's run from there, as we drove into that little town it was like going home.

Back to our holiday again, we were told there was a festival being held in Sitges, , a sight not to be missed. We told them in the hotel we would be back about 9pm and they said a meal would be waiting for us. They gave us a packed lunch and away we went. We had to drive through Barcelona, towards the docks was a big island with a huge statue of Christopher Columbus and we knew we had to turn off at this island, but Sitges wasn't signposted. After circling this island four times we at last made someone understand and we had to take the Girona road. We got to sitges, all roads in the town were closed to traffic, we managed to find a parking space on the outside of the town. All the streets were long carpets of flowers, all carnations, dyed and formed into a pattern. One street was flags of all nations, we found the Union Jack, it was a marvellous site and after tramping around the streets we went on to the sea front, a lovely promenade and a beautiful white sandy beach. After a cup of tea in a cafe it was time to start back.

That's when our trouble started, we couldn't find the car. All I could remember it was by an orchard, it was two hours later we found it, of course this made us late starting back and it gets dark early in Spain, and most of the roads were just dirt tracks in them days. We were almost back when we came to a full stop, there was a big pole across the road with Diversion wrote across it, a motor bike passed us, turned down a dirt track and we followed him. It led into a large sweetcorn plantation, it was like going into a hop yard, and the further we went the narrower the furrow (??) became, until we could go no further, we were stuck in a rut. Stan left me in the car while he went searching for something to put under the back wheel. It was pitch dark and I was scared stiff. He wasn't away long, he had found an old sack, pushed it under the wheel and got back on to the main road again. It was ten o clock when we reached the hotel, the staff were worried, couldn't think what had happened to us, and were allowed in the dining room for a hot meal.

The day before we were to start back it was my 50th birthday. When we came down for breakfast the proprietor's wife presented me with a beautiful bouquet of flowers and a large cut glass vase to put them in. After breakfast Stan said I am taking you on a boat trip today, it was market day and there were stalls the whole length of the promenade, stopping at a jewellery stall he bought me a lovely watch. Then we went for the boat, sat on the top deck and cruised along the Costa Brava coastline as far as San Felu, returning to Blanes at 5pm. Our Dutch friends were waiting for us on the beach and we treated them to strawberries and ice cream back at the hotel. Late that night when it was quiet in the bar, Stan bought the bartender and waitress a drink, they put on music and danced, the end of a perfect day.

We had an uneventful journey back, we travelled from the middle of France, right on to a ferry at Boulogne. On reaching England he said "I'm not stopping again, with a bit of luck, we will get to the Hundred House by 10pm." He was dying for a pint of English beer. We arrived just as they were about to put the towel on, everybody wanted to hear about our holiday. We eventually went home, Stan drove straight into the garage and I told him to leave everything as it was too late and I was too tired to do any unpacking. Stan was going through the pile of mail when he said "there's a letter for you". Opening it he said you have won £50 on some bonds, and for a minute I couldn't think what he was talking about. He gave me the letter and the penny dropped, it was a win on the Premium bonds, but I said it isn't £50 it's £500, and

50 years ago that was a lot of money. I was so excited I couldn't sleep when I went to bed. We were having tea the next night when Mary my niece called to tell us Howard had died in the ambulance on the way to hospital. It was a shock, but what a blessing he didn't go on holiday with us. I went to see Molly, but I didn't say a word about my windfall, and not long after her eldest son died from a brain haemorrhage. Poor Molly, her world fell apart.

The next year we decided to try the Atlantic side of Spain, we had made friends with one of Mander's reps, he was married to a Spanish girl, Paquita, they had a 3 months old baby boy. Her parents lived in Pampiona and she hadn't seen them for four years. Could they come with us? Stan agreed to take them, so plans went ahead. Paquita went for advice from the doctor about the baby, who turned down the idea, saying it would have had to have all injections and was too young. Then Bob's mother said she would have the baby, Paquita was so excited, she bought presents for all her family and was so looking forward to seeing them all. Then a fortnight before our departure her mother-in-law changed her mind regarding the baby. The poor girl was heartbroken, we agreed to try and find her parents, she gave us all the presents she had bought, and slides and viewer, so that her parents would be able to see what her home and baby looked like.

So off we went on our own, we sailed from Southampton to Cherbourg on a midnight boat, we had reclining chairs and a red blanket, so we slept during the crossing. We arrived at Cherbourg at 4.30am but were not allowed to disembark until 5am. This gave us time to have a wash and a drink before starting on our long journey. We reached San Sebastian by tea time, it was a big port and I remember having coffee at a café on the quayside. A few miles further on we came to a small resort called Zarouz, found a nice hotel and booked in. After our evening meal we decided to go down to the sea front, we found a short cut which led down to the beach. It was a lovely long white sandy beach, but deserted, I was soon to know why. I stepped over the low sea wall on to the sand, my feet began to sink, beneath was thick black oil. It was the year of the oil tanker Torre Canyon disaster, the oil had swept all along that coastline and the incoming tides had covered it with sand. I managed to find a piece of glass and cleaned my shoes as best I could. All day on the Sunday we had a terrible thunderstorm, Stan said we're moving out of here and we are not coming back. So the next morning we set off for Pamplona, reached the town at mid day, we had a post card with the address clearly written on it. We stopped several people, who shook their heads, we couldn't understand their directions. We found a parking space, it was a very busy town with crowds of people around, we sat in the car, not knowing what to do. We had all the windows open as it was terribly hot, after a while I saw a man in a brown cassock walking down the street, I thought, he's a priest and he'll surely know the area. Stan beckoned him over and he spoke English. We had quite a long chat, he wrote the directions down for us and before leaving, he put his arm around Stan's shoulders and said "you are many miles from home, God be with you on your journey". I had never given it a thought how far from home we were before and for a priest to come to our rescue, it made me think there was someone up above looking after us.

We found the flats and Stan went up, came back down clutching the girl's hand, she must have thought she was being abducted. I just said "Paquita, Anglaise" and she understood. She became so excited and was jabbering away, neither of us understanding what the other was saying. We gathered all the presents and went up to the flat and met her Mamma and Pappa, and when they saw all the presents they knew we were genuine friends and made us so welcome. In Spain all the family go to their parents for lunch, the married daughter arrived with her baby and husband, then their two sons came in from work. They all dined in the kitchen, their Mom laid a small table in the sitting room for Stan and I and put on a lovely meal for us. After lunch Mamma put on her new dress that Paquita had sent and Papa his new black beret. I took a snap of them together and they couldn't stop looking at the slides of Paquita and her baby.

We spent three lovely hours with them and they all came out and waved goodbye. They filled our water carrier and Stan stopped at a garage and topped up with petrol and we were away, intending to cross to the other side of Spain. We got on to a new highway and we travelled mile after mile. It was like driving through a desert, from one horizon to the other, just sun baked clay which looked like sand, not a blade of grass or tree, we had to keep going. At last we passed a signpost, 100 kilometres Motel, we gave a sigh of relief, with a bit of luck we would put up for the night. It was a very old, isolated hotel, on the front was a large compound with live stags wondering around, it must have been an old coach house years before but we had no choice but to book in.

There was a row of old two storey buildings with large garage doors, they gave us keys and pointed to where we were to go, nobody spoke English. Stan drove in and we climbed stone steps which led into a bedroom above. I inspected the bed, that was alright, on each wall was a stag's head and rush mats on the floor, very queer. But we had a surprise, leading off the bedroom was a lovely tiled bathroom. We had food and everything for our use in the car below. I opened a tin of corned beef and cooked chips, we didn't fancy going into the hotel and we were away early the next morning. Reaching Barcelona early afternoon and on to Blanes to our favourite hotel, we were welcome with open arms and stayed for the rest of the holiday.

The next year we decided to go to Italy, we booked the ferry from Dover to Ostend and stayed at at a motel in the middle of France and away early the next morning. No motorways had yet been built and we drove through all the big towns en route. I saw a signpost for Grenoble and said I'd love to see where they did the skiing. Leaving Grenoble we were in the French Alps having left our main route, we didn't know where we were but we had to keep going, terrible hairpin bends and no barriers on the outside. Darkness fell and we were still up in these mountains. Stan pulled up, we could hear a bell clanging, a man came into view carrying a lantern and ringing a bell, behind him a flock of sheep. Another car had pulled up behind us and when the sheep had passed the fellow in the other car came over to speak to us, he said he had tailed us for hours, and heading for Nice, travelling overnight. We had no intention of travelling all night if we could find somewhere to stay, but it was nice to know we were not alone on that mountain.

We eventually came to the bottom and there was a hotel, Stan jumped out of the car and booked in. The other car pulled in at the side of us, they were a young English couple and undecided what to do, I asked the girl if she was scared on that mountain. She said she was terrified and so was I and I said whatever was around the corner it was best to tackle it in daylight. They booked in too, they must have had a very early start next morning as we didn't see them again. We arrived on the sea front of Nice early afternoon, after a quick look round, we carried on to Monaco, saw Prince Rainier's palace, then drove into Monte Carlo, stopping right in front of the Casino. Not knowing where we were allowed to park, Stan beckoned a policeman over, he was dressed immaculate, white helmet, gloves and shoes and chocolate brown uniform. He thought we wanted the casino, Stan said no casino and with a little miming he understood, so we parked and went to the harbour, everywhere was beautiful but we had to move on though.

Monaco and into Italy, it had been a coastal road all the way from Nice, it was lovely. We had been recommended a hotel in Alasio, but they were fully booked, but they had a new hotel a little way down the Promenade, we found it and booked in for seven days. Walking along the Prom the next morning, Stan seemed worried, he was trying to reckon up what it would cost to stay at this hotel, it was thousands of lire and we had to allow for the journey home. So we went back to the hotel and after reckoning up all our money and allowing for any unforeseen expense we could just about afford to stay, so I said right I'll be a lady for a week. The hotel was fabulous, with its own private beach, but there was something lacking, Italians are not as friendly as Spanish people.

The week soon passed and it was time to hit the trail again. The first night we stayed at a hotel in Stresa on the shore of Lake Maggiore, away early next morning heading for Lucerne, we travelled the whole length of Lake Maggiore, the road winds alongside the lake the whole way, the scenery was out of this world. We were in mountains again, heading for the Bernard pass instead of driving over the top. We found out we could go by rail through a tunnel and give Stan a rest from driving. One minute we were in bright sunshine and the next in total darkness, so Stan turned on our interior lights and one by one the other cars did the same. Coming out of the mountain we headed for Lucerne and stayed the night in a hotel beside the lake. After breakfast the next morning we were on our travels again, heading for Basle. But Stan took the wrong turning and we finished up in Innsbruck in Austria, miles out of our way. But the scenery was beautiful and Stan said he wouldn't have missed it for anything. We stopped for a short break and headed for France, staying overnight at a place called Beaune. Next day going through Chartres we passed right beside the Notre Dame cathedral, so I asked Stan to stop as I would like to go inside. After climbing a lot of steps we entered by a side door, it was massive, large stone archways and beautiful music was being played. We walked on and on and stopping to look through one of these arches, there before the High Altar was a coffin on a catafalque and the mourners were walking around, we lit a candle and left, arriving home safe after another adventurous holiday.

We always went to Blackpool in Spetember for the illuminations and I must record this one year. There were seven of us, Jack and Jose, Josie's brother and his girlfriend in Jack's car, Stan and I in ours and Colin on his motorbike. We started off just after tea on the Friday night, everything was fine until it started to rain and it poured down for mile after mile. Stan was worried about Colin on his bike, I think it was Wigan where we stopped and Jack offered to give Colin a break, so he put on Colin's leathers and Alan drove Jack's car and away we went, arriving in Blackpool, still pouring with rain. We went up North to the hotel where we normally stayed, she was fully booked. She gave us several addresses and if we couldn't get in anywhere, to go back and she would accommodate us somehow. We had no luck, it was getting late and still raining, so we went back. Joan, Josie and I shared a small back bedroom and she made makeshift beds for the men on the dining room floor, but at least we were all under the same roof. We had to be up very early the next morning, had breakfast and away before the other guests came down. We spent a few hours in Blackpool and left, we had had enough. What a smashing trip that was!

I was still working at Golfars but one Saturday morning looking through the County Express I saw an advertisement for machinists. Sid Griffiths, who still (had) a large garage on the Hayes, was opening up as a sideline in dressing gowns, so off I went for an interview and got the job. We were paid daywork and it was as much as I could earn piecework at Golfars, so I put in my notice and left. It was great, everything was new, even to a new pair of scissors. There were only ten machinists, each one of us had a special job, I put the collars on, it was a doddle, at the end of the line the garments were finished. On the other side of the room was a large long table on which the cutting out was done. It was fascinating to watch Terry, an experienced cutter laying out the bales of cloth, the garments were cut out in dozens with an electric blade. Our hours were 8.30 till 4.30 with a 15 minute break at 10 a.m. The forewoman would make us a cup of tea and three quarters of an hour for lunch. On our first day the power was switched off at 4 p.m, and Sid the boss came in carrying a large box of drinking glasses and bottles of champagne and so we toasted the success of his company, what a lovely start to a new job.

At Christmas we all had five pounds bonus, he laid a white sheet on the bottom end of the cutting table, put on a buffet for us, had a turkey delivered from Taylor's bakery, donned a chef's hat and did the carving. All kinds of spirits, Mr Coyle, a buyer from Birmingham came and gave us all a present. we had a smashing time.

As the year wore on, holidays was the topic, we were planning to go to Spain again, and two teenagers, Margaret and June, said they would love to come with us, so I told them if they could get their parent's consent, I was sure Stan would take them. They were that excited, never been abroad, and June, who was an only child, arranged for us to meet her parents. She lived in Netherton and having met us, they agreed to let her go. Her Mom and Dad came down to Southampton to see us off. I had written to Blanes and booked a suite at a different hotel so we were sure of our accommodation. We stayed at a motel overnight, cooked breakfast on the side of the road, the girls thought it was great, and away again. We were travelling through the Lot country which is a very pretty part of France, and pulled up on a scenic lay-by. We had just started to move away when a car travelling at speed came round a bend, when bang, we had a shattered windscreen. Stan slowly bought the car to a stop, we got out as the glass continued to fall, a passing car, seeing our predicament, pulled up and the fellow came with a wooden mallet and helped Stan remove the loose glass, our next problem, where to get a new windscreen. I got in the back of the car with the girls as bits of glass continued to fall, we got as far as Carcassonne, pulled in to a large garage, our luck was in, they had a windscreen. In half an hour they vacuumed all the glass out of the car and fixed the new one in. When we came to pay we hadn't enough Francs to pay in French money, no problem on our part, Stan offered him a traveller's cheque, which he refused to accept until had checked it out with the bank. The bank was closed for lunch so it was one and a half hours later we started away. With all this delay we were well out of our time schedule, we should have been at the hotel in time for our evening meal. Anyway, we decided to stop, so we pulled on to a grass verge at the side of a river, made a pot of tea and had something to eat. There was a car next to ours and I noticed they had a GB on the back of the car, so I went over to them, they were a young couple with two small children. They were going to Barcelona, so I asked if they were hoping to cross the border, which in those days was at the top of a mountain, only one more hour to go, and as we drove into that small town, Blanes, it was like going home.

The proprietor and his wife were sitting under the trees on the promenade, waiting for us. The suite was lovely, two bedrooms and bathroom, we had a balcony leading off our bedroom and as we were on the third floor, we had a lovely view of the harbour, sea and all along the promenade. I told the girls our bedroom door would never be shut and they were free to use the balcony as they wished. We had a smashing holiday, they never gave us a minute's worry and they got on so well with Stan. We took them on boat trips and one night we hired a taxi and took them to a nightclub in Lloret. I haven't seen them for years, but I bet they have never forgotten that holiday.

We returned home without any mishaps, June's mom, dad, gran and granddad were on the quay side when we docked, so glad to see June safely back. The next year it was Spain again, taking Gladys and Arthur Rimmer with us. Arthur's younger brother had been killed during the war and was buried in the Canadian cemetery near Cairn, so on the way back we visited it and found his grave. It's a beautiful cemetery, on the other hand heartbreaking, so many young lives lost, lads only eighteen years old and some known only to God. That was the highlight of that holiday.

As we were both getting older, I told Stan it was time to cut out all this travelling by car, and went by air. He wasn't very impressed, however we went to Blackpool for the lights. After tea he went out to the car, when I joined him he had two elderly ladies in the back, while waiting for me he had got chatting to them, they said they were going to walk down to the front to see the lights, so Stan offered to take them with us. We were staying at a hotel up North and had to get down to Squires Gate to join the queue. On the way down he saw a signpost to the airport and decided to go and have a look round. We found it, parked and went inside the reception. On a notice board there was a day trip by plane to the Isle of Man. The next day, Stan went and booked it, my inside turned over every time I thought of where I was going the next day, they were small planes. Back at the hotel the ladies thanked us for a lovely night out and we told the landlady of our plans for the next day. She said she would give us a packed lunch and have a hot meal for us on our return. Stan said he would skip breakfast, she said "Oh no you won't, I shall bring you a tablet to calm you down". The next morning he was in a right old state, had to keep dashing to the toilet. I thought we would never make it but we did, as soon as we were airborne he was OK. There was a bus waiting to take us into Douglas, the place was deserted, all shops were closed and nearly all hotels on the sea front were boarded up and the beach was horrible. I was never so disappointed, walking along the front we met one couple only, I recognised them, they came from of all places, Lye! We stopped, chatting, they were on a fortnight's holiday. We had a ride on the horse drawn tram, we were the only people on it and I was glad when it was time to get the plane back, at least we had overcome the fear of flying. There were to be many changes in our lives, it was January and Stan seldom had work at that time of year. We were in the Liberal club and a fellow came over to Stan and told him they needed a painter at the Bronx (engineering company in Lye), so knocking five years off his age, he got it, the easiest job he'd ever had, painting machinery.

It was Easter, we had had two days holiday, on the Wednesday morning when we started back at Golfar's at 10.30 all the power was turned off and the boss came in to talk to us. The company had gone into liquidation, we were to finish off the garments and that was it, we were all made redundant. It was such a shock to all of us, we had threehappy years there. On the Saturday morning I was reading the Country Express when I saw an advert, a vending machine attendant needed at Helix in Engine Lane. I knew nothing about these machines but I had nothing to lose, so off I went, I got an appointment to see the personnel officer on the Monday morning. Stan was dead against me going but I was determined to see it through, so I went for the interview. I confessed I had never seen the inside of a vending machine and as there was one in every department he took me all around the factory and introduced me to Ken Hamblett, who was to teach me. In the canteen, he introduced me to the staff as Ellen. I would have to serve tea, sweets and cigarettes to the workers at lunch time. We went back to Mr Waller's office to talk it over. Mr Waller was a very nice elderly gentleman, and I decided to give it a go. The nurse bought me a coffee and took me by car into Stourbridge as I was going shopping. I was given VIP treatment and I started the next day. Ken supervised me with two machines, then left me to do the third on my own. There were seven machines all in different departments, I got carried away. I knew I had to be in the canteen at 12.15 when I eventually found it, the workers had already had their lunch break and were back at work. Mr Waller came into the canteen and I apologised, he told me to get a sweet and have my lunch break, so I went and got myself a dish of rice pudding and custard. My hours were 8am till 2pm. Stan never asked me how I got on, I had gone against his wishes and didn't want to know. I couldn't understand his objection when everyone was so nice to me, the pay was good, I had only been there six weeks and I was paid a full week's holiday money at Whitsun.

The factory closed down in August for a fortnight, so we took our first holiday by plane to Cala Millor in Majorca, it was beautiful, lovely beaches. One day we went on a mini cruise and passed by the Kennedy's residence and Harry Secombe's, of course they had private beaches and no outsiders were allowed to land. Further on around the coastline we pulled into a little cove, the boatman told us where we could find a small café, and they wanted us back in one hour. So we all wondered off through the woods, we found it and by the time we had all been served it was time to return. While we were away the boatman had got a barbecue going for us in an open space, just inside the wood. Tables were laid to help ourselves, free sangria and four musicians. The young ones sang and danced the afternoon away, a very enjoyable day.

Back home again, a huge redevelopment plan was in progress, all properties on Waste Bank, Cross Walks and Upper High Street were to be demolished, our house included. Mrs Homer sold our houses to the Council, bought a house in King Street and moved out. We had to let the council know which area we wished to be re housed, we didn't have much choice, it was either Stambermill or Wynall, so we settled for Wynall. Mr Bayliss the housing manager sent us a letter offering us three houses, we went up after tea and Stan said Number four Oakfield Road seemed the most suitable. I went for the keys and a friend came with me to see it, I was terribly disappointed. I was expecting a nice bathroom, instead there was an old cankered bath on rusty iron legs, an old fashioned toilet, no sink unit in the kitchen, just a small square sink. I didn't feel like accepting it, anyway Stan was determined to see it so we went up after tea, taking a pair of steps. After looking around we were in the living room, he got the steps and started fiddling with the paper over the front window. Suddenly the whole ceiling paper came down on top of me, Stan laughed, said he had never stripped a ceiling so quick. I went to see Mr Bayliss the next day and he promised to put in a new bath, wash basin, toilet and a new kitchen window. Any other work we would have to pay for, I said I would like the middle wall knocked out of the kitchen, we were willing to pay so providing we employed workmen on their books he gave us consent, also to make a drive. Harold Charnock came and dug up part of the hedge and lawn for the drive, the wall was knocked out, all the kitchen plastered and Stan painted and decorated throughout. We moved in during our August holidays, after living on a High Street for thirty four years it was like being in another world. Our working hours corresponded and Stan dropped me off at Helix on his way to the Bronx. We had two more holidays abroad by plane, first to Salou and the last to Blanes, but our good times were not to last much longer.

We had a phone call from Marj, Tom was seriously ill and was going into St Thomas' hospital in London for open heart surgery. It was a terribly worrying time but he pulled through. He was there six weeks then moved to a hospital in Poole. Marj rang and asked if I would go down and spend the weekend with her, so I packed a suitcase, took it to work with me on the Friday morning and caught the 2.15pm train from Lye station into Birmingham, where I caught a through train to Bournemouth, Marj was there to meet me. We went straight to the hospital, Tom was so pleased to see me and he wanted to come home with us, so to pacify him Marj said she would bring his clothes if the hospital would discharge him. But they wouldn't give their consent so we spent most of the weekend visiting him. I left after lunch on Sunday, Judith came with me to the station to see me off, we got to Eastleigh and all had to get off and on to coaches that were waiting to take us to another station, the train lines were being repaired. I had to change again twice and it was ten o'clock when I got to Birmingham. I decided to go for a number nine bus, only to see the back of one going out which meant another twenty minutes wait. It was 11.15 when I got into Lye. I thought I would ring Stan to come and pick me up, but I hadn't any change, so there was no alternative, I would have to walk up to Wynall, the last bus had gone. I had a large picture which Marj had bought me, plus my suitcase, and my shoes were crippling me, so I took them off and walked barefoot home. Was Stan glad to see me, he immediately rang Marj to let her know I had arrived safe, Tom made a wonderful recovery.

Back to Helix, I was in the canteen waiting for the workers to arrive, outside there was an elderly man washing the boss' car, it was a bitterly cold day and he looked perished, so I knocked the window and beckoned him in and gave him a cup of tea. Bill was a good friend to me later on. Apart from helping in the canteen and cleaning and maintaining the machines, I would be called for over the intercom. One day a girl came over to me and just stood, staring at me, she said "Don't you recognise me?". Her face seemed familiar so I asked if we had worked together somewhere, she said no, "You're my auntie Nell", it was June, I hadn't seen her since she was a child, now she was a married woman. It was hearing my name over the intercom that got her wondering could I be a relative. It was a lovely surprise, June had got a cushy job, counting and packing rulers, education items were made there and distributed all over the world and is still a well known firm today.

My brother Stan had a stroke, leaving his right arm paralysed, and Fred wasn't well, it was six months later, we both went to work as normal, in the afternoon I stopped to do shopping in Lye, making me later than usual getting home. Mrs Scott, a neighbour, was looking out for me, a man from the Bronx had called and left a message, I was to ring the Bronx immediately. My first thoughts were there had been an accident, but when I rang they told me Stan had been taken ill and taken to Corbett hospital, and they came and took me to see him. He had had a stroke and was still semi-concious. I didn't stay long, they told me to come later, the man from the Bronx had waited for me and took me home. Colin was in Scotland at Glasgow University, studying for a degree, and I felt there was no point in ringing him straight away. I made myself a cup of tea and someone was knocking the door, it was Tom, he had come up from Bournemouth for a week's holiday and was staying with Marj's Mom. Was I glad to see him, I knew he would help me, he took me to the hospital every night. I went into work on the Monday and told Ken I would have to have time off when Stan came home. He said not to worry, he would look after the machines and Bill offered to run me up to the hospital straight from work in the afternoons. A week later Stan came home, he had recovered quite well, but he had lost part of the use of his right hand and leg. Mr Scott had helped me to get the bed down into the front room. The first night at home, he woke me up in the middle of the night, he'd cooked my breakfast, bacon, egg and a thick piece of bread. I looked at the clock, it was 2.30. I sat up in bed and forced it down, I didn't say anything to upset him, he was that pleased he had been able to do it for me, it was something he'd done for years, but of course the timing was wrong.

His general health improved but I knew he would never work again, so back I went to Helix. Bill picked me up in the morning and ran me home at 2pm, thus saving me a lot of time and bus fare. I applied for home work and they delivered 5 bags of small compasses, which had to have a washer screwed on. Stan slipped on the washers and I screwed them on at night. It was the best thing I could have done, it acted as a therapy and brought the use back into his hand and he was so proud to get a pay packet at the end of the week. So life went on, Colin had got his degree and wanted us to go up for his graduation. I went to see the doctor for his advice, he said whatever has got to happen will happen, and if you stay at home and nothing has happened, you missed out on a lot of pleasure, so go.

Bill took us to the station and promised to meet us at New Street station on our return. Colin was waiting for us in Glasgow, hired a taxi to the hotel that he had previously booked near to the university. Stan was shattered and had to go to bed, Colin came into the dining room before we had finished breakfast. The next morning we went by train to Windermere and had a four hour cruise on the lake, Stan loved going on boats and it was a beautiful day. The next day we spent at the university and after the ceremonies there was a buffet, so it filled in our second day. The next day he took us by taxi to the station and went by train to Greenock, where we got on a boat over the Clyde to Dunoon. So ended a most enjoyable stay in Glasgow, Bill was waiting for us in Birmingham and took us home.

Back to Helix, it was sometime later I was called to the personnel office to be told that the canteen staff and I were to be made redundant, as it had been decided to have outside catering. He said I could reapply but they didn't pay so much, so I told him, no way would I do the same job for less money. He offered me an early morning cleaning job, 7 – 9am, and thinking it over I took it, apart from the early start at least I would be with Stan all day. It was clean work, in the main office, there were two of us, Edna would start one end and me the other, we had twenty five office desks to polish then Hoover the whole area. In the centre was a fish pond and fountain, a beautiful office. It was then I met Hilda and we became friends, she cleaned other offices. Hilda and her husband Fred would come over on a Saturday night and take us to the Greyhound in Norton. Stan was only allowed two halves of shandy but he didn't mind as he enjoyed the company.

Bill's wife passed away and he would join us too, I had worked at Helix for five years and employees were given awards for every five years service. Everybody had to assemble in the canteen, and having been tea lady I was known by everyone and as I walked up to the stage the applause was deafening, I felt so embarrassed. I bought a china tea set with my cheque from Boots in Stourbridge, but life was not to go smoothly for long. Stan's mom passed away, she was in her ninetieth year, leaving an unmarried brother and sister, Harry and Doris, who had never got on. Doris was an alcoholic and hated Harry, but he had a lady friend so he had some pleasure in life, although he was in poor health. I still carried on with my early morning job and coming up Lye one morning who should be sitting on the seat by Lye church was Harry, he looked dreadful. He had been to see his doctor, who had prescribed a bottle of cough mixture. I begged him to come back home with me, but no, he said he would go home and go to bed. At tea time I had a phone call from Dorothy, his lady friend, and she was in tears. She cleaned the bank on Lye Cross and on her way down had called to see Harry, she was so upset and thought he was dying, so I told her I would get help somehow. Putting the phone down I thought now what am I going to do, the only thing I could think of was to call an ambulance and get him to hospital. I had to explain to Stan what I was about to do, we had had our tea and he said he would be alright to be left and not to worry. If I was away a long time I would ring him from the hospital. I rang Corbett's gave them all the particulars, he had seen the doctor that morning but now had terrible pain across his chest. I now had to get down to Harry's as quick as I could, a neighbour ran me down by car, the ambulance was already there and I went with him. I sat in a corridor outside the room where they had taken Harry, at about 8pm, a nurse bought me a cup of tea and told me he was being admitted and needed immediate surgery, I would be able to see him before going into the ward. I phoned Stan and Ken my next door neighbour saw me dash off and came to see what was wrong and was staying with Stan, so that was a relief, and back I went to wait again. It was 9.30 when I was called in, he was so upset tears rolled down his cheeks and I tried to console him. I was given a carrier bag with all his clothes and possessions, and he asked me to promise not to let anyone have his keys. I knew what he meant, I managed to get the last bus up to Wynall. What had I let myself in for? I phoned from work the next morning, he had had his operation and was comfortable.

Waiting for me on Lye Cross was Doris, she wanted to come back with me for his clothes, it wasn't his clothes she wanted, it was his wallet. I told her I was sorry but Harry had told me to take care of everything, she was mad but I didn't care, I knew her too well. He continued to improve but he was worried, he had a large amount of money locked up in the wardrobe and if Doris could get her hands on it, it would be the last he would see of it, so could I somehow get it out. I talked it over with his brother Bill and it was arranged for Bill's wife Betty to take Doris to the hospital, so Bill and I went down to the house. Bill had bought a big torch, it was dark but we didn't switch on any lights, Harry had put a big padlock on the wardrobe door, but no problem, I had the keys. We did a thorough search, old photographs, documents and money all went into my shopping bag, locked up and left. Bill came back home with me, we counted all his money and I paid it into Harry's account the next day. What a strange experience, but was Harry pleased when he saw his bank book. He made a reasonable recovery and came home. Christmas came around, I went down to see him, Dorothy was there and they were looking through holiday brochures, he was planning to take her abroad. But sadly that wasn't to be and at the end of February he passed away.

It was summer again, a lovely sunny morning, and Stan sat in the front doorway, while I went to fetch him a newspaper. Coming back, I told him to go and sit in the lounge, he said "Nell, I can't see", thinking it was coming out of the bright sunshine I helped him into his chair. I went into the kitchen to cook our dinner and calling him when he was ready, he said "Nell I still can't see", I knew something was wrong. His doctor came to see him and said he would arrange for us to go to Birmingham eye hospital. I was told the sun had shattered all the blood vessels in the back of his eyes and there was nothing they could do. I now had a full time job looking after him, there was no outside help in those days, but I had a lot to be thankful for, he was good tempered and thanked me for every little thing I did for him. I got in touch with Mrs Bridgewater, who ran a handicap club in Norton, it was only one night a month but something for us to look forward to. Roger, a doctor's son from Halesowen would come and pick us up in his car, and fetched us back at 9pm. On our return he would come in, I would make a pot of tea, he loved his cup of tea, and chocolate biscuits, and he would stay for half an hour. He was a lovely lad and came whatever the weather. He did it on a voluntary basis and we became good friends.

Life never ran smoothly for long, Stan had a heart attack, I rang for an ambulance, they came immediately and took him to Corbett's. They were short staffed and Stan was a problem, the Sister asked me if I would go up and help him at mealtimes. He was there one week and recovered reasonably well. My brother Fred was seriously ill, I didn't visit as often as I would have liked, as my only free time was if Stan went to bed afternoons. I happened to go on his last day on Earth, memories are too sad to record. Mary his daughter ran me home, she was in tears, having recently lost her husband, he was only 37 years old, and she had three young children. Her Dad passed away that same night. They say trouble never comes in ones, they were coming to me in cartloads, and still more to come.

Colin moved down to Cranfield from Scotland, he had secured a place at the Institute for Technology and Science, studying for a Degree, so we saw very little of him, he did keep in touch by phone. It was down there he met Janet, they came to see us at Christmas and were getting married in the February. Jan had her own flat near Wembley Stadium and the wedding was to be in London and he wanted us both to go. When I took him to Scotland Stan had his sight, no way could I take him to London on my own, then I had a brainwave. I rang Hilda and Fred, I asked if they would like a day out in London, all expenses paid, and they readily agreed. So we went, Stan was so pleased, he knew Fred would look after him. Colin sent us an itinerary and we found the flat without problems. All Jan's family had travelled down from Yorkshire the day before. It was a registry wedding, the wedding was held at a pub, they had invited all their friends and their children and a lovely meal was served. At tea time Col and Jan left for an unknown destination and we all prepared to go home. It had been a lovely day and Fred and Hilda had really enjoyed it.

Colin and Jan left London, bought a little alms house in Saffron Walden, very quaint, and a lovely little market town. Colin got through all his exams and he got two of their friends from Willenhall to take us down for the passing out ceremony. He was now a Doctor of Philosophy, soon found work and Jan was expecting. I was now in my sixties and had given up hope of ever having a grandchild, I was delighted, had something to look forward to. She was born June 26th, it was eleven o clock at night and we had gone to bed when the phone rang. It was Colin, telling us we had a granddaughter, she was half an hour old, I had little sleep that night. She was christened in Jan's family Catholic church in Bradford, Colin fetched us up there for the ceremony, we stayed with Jan's Mom overnight, going back home the next day. It was sad, Stan couldn't see his granddaughter.

So life went on, Bill had retired from Helix and would come over every Wednesday afternoon and take me to Asda in Brierley Hill for all my weekly shopping, he gave me all the help he could during those troublesome years. My brother Stan passed away in Hayley Green and my Stan had another heart attack and he was back in hospital again. It was summer time and the council had decided all houses in our area were to be modernised. They came to see me and offered me other accommodation, which I refused. Stan would have been more confused than he already was, so I settled for a caravan on the drive. Work started the beginning of august, all carpets and furniture went into storage, I was left with Stan's armchair, fridge, TV and our bed, we had to sleep in the house at night. The caravan was lovely, a bunk bed where Stan could have a rest every afternoon, a wardrobe for our clothes and a small grill with two hobs. We had to wake up early in a morning and in the caravan before 8am. The workmen worked from 8am till 6pm, washing was my biggest problem, they disconnected everything in the kitchen, my washer, stove and fridge were all put in the front room. They provided me with a small water heater and I did my washing in a bowl on top of the dustbin outside. They didn't concentrate on one house, they worked in every house along the road, so we were all in the same predicament. There was only one thing in our favour, it was beautiful weather. Nothing went right for me, a fellow went in one day and knocked all the ceiling off the toilet, left all the rubbish for me to clean up, sprayed all the house with Rentokil, only to find out he was in the wrong house.

Another night the workmen had gone, leaving the overflow running like a fountain over the back door, so I went next door and asked Tony if he could do something about it. We went upstairs to the airing cupboard and turned off all taps. I now had no water at all, turning round to go out of the room, we found the whole wall of plaster had fallen down. Tony said "get me a shovel and plastic bags and I'll get it up for you". I had run out of plastic bags, so we decided to get the bed into the other room. I had covered the bed with dust sheets so no plaster had got into the bed, and the fellow that had knocked it down had to get it up. Every night after they had gone I had to sweep up and brush the stairs down before I could get Stan into the house, we had no bath for five weeks.

Looking back I don't know how I coped, it was November, fourteen weeks from when they had started, they came and switched the central heating on so I told Stan he could go to bed for his afternoon nap, and as I was getting him upstairs I saw water pouring from the light in the spare bedroom. I got a dust sheet, put it on the floor and dashed down to the workmen's hut. They told me to go back and turn every tap off in the airing cupboard, it was lunch hour and they would be along later. A fellow came in the afternoon, said he was putting in a brand new tank, so I said was the other someone's old one? I was mad, decorators had to come back again, eventually everything was back to normal. Jan, Kathryn and Colin spent Christmas with us that year. It was February 18th, Jan's birthday, the phone rang at lunchtime, it was Colin, telling me his firm had laid him off as they had closed his section down.. They had moved into a detached house, taken out a higher mortgage and Jan was now pregnant. I tried to keep the news from Stan, but he kept asking why Colin had phoned, so I told him. We were both worried but nothing we could do, it was Friday and Colin always rang us Sunday nights so we hadn't long to wait before we were in touch again.

Sunday morning Stan wasn't well, had pains in his stomach, I was worried. My hot water bottle had sprung a leak, I borrowed one from my friend Minnie who lived opposite, but it had no effect, so the day wore on. Minnie came over and advised me to send for the doctor, his own doctor was off duty and a lady doctor came, and while she was examining him he had a nasty turn, she thought he was having a fit. After quietening down she made him more comfortable and said he would sleep for two or three hours and I was to get the bed downstairs. I went over the road and asked Mr Scott to help me, between us we got it down and they both left. Minnie, who had a coal fire, was worried in case it had gone out, and I continued making up the bed, I kept looking across at Stan, he looked strange. I put my hand inside his shirt, there was no heartbeat, I realised he'd gone. As I went to phone it was ringing in, it was Colin, I told him I thought his Dad had passed away and must ring the doctor to confirm it. She came, it was true, the phone rang, she answered it, it was Colin, and she told me he would be with me around midnight. Minnie got in touch with the undertaker, and at 9pm Stan was taken away. What a day it had been, left on my own, my thoughts were with Colin, making that long journey from Saffron Walden, and after his own worries the last two days, was I glad when he arrived safely. He took over, made all necessary arrangements, stayed three days, then had to go home to fetch Jan and the child for the funeral. Meantime Tom and Marj had come up from Bournemouth, so I was never on my own during the day, and they stayed for a fortnight. I had to do so much for Stan, I didn't know what to do with my time. I gave all his clothes and donations to the handicapped club and it was sometime later I got an invitation from them to go to dinner down Kinver. I accepted and they fetched me. During the evening Freda Sunter, (she ran the Dudley disabled holiday group) announced she was planning a holiday to Majorca, if anyone was interested. So when she came to our table I asked if I could go too. She agreed, I would be classed as an escort, and I now had something to look forward to. I joined the Evergreen Club in Wollescote, and the afternoon class at the Salvation Army in Lye, meeting up with old friends. I hadn't seen Bill for weeks, curiosity got the better of me and I decided I would find out what had become of him. I had never been to Blackheath but I found the street, I knocked the side door, no answer, the woman next door must have seen me, she came and told me Mr Newman was in Dudley Guest Hospital so on the Saturday afternoon I went to visit him. He was glad to see me, he had a bad ulcerated leg and had a big skin graft. I visited him Saturday afternoons, it found me somewhere to go and cheered him up. He was there for ten months.

Meantime arrangements were going ahead for our holiday, I was to share a room with a lady from Netherton, they had given my phone number and she phoned me. Her name was Isabel, but known as Ellie. We were to meet for the first time at the airport, I asked how I would recognise her, she said "You won't miss me I'm 16 stone". She had never been abroad and was so excited. We went to Ca'n Pastilla, it was lovely, beautiful beach and promenade, we stayed at a hotel on the sea front and I remember the first time we went on to our balcony Ellie was spellbound and she was happy if she had to spend all her holiday just sitting there. Her only problem was she couldn't walk very far, they had taken a wheelchair for her, so two afternoons I took her out and pushed her from one end of the prom to the other. She had to get out when we came to gutters, no way could I have lifted her up. She couldn't thank me enough, we had a wonderful holiday, they were such a happy crowd.

Back home again I missed Stan terribly, but I had a cat, Sandy, to welcome me, a neighbour had looked after him, if I went out he would be by the gate waiting for me to return, he was such a good companion. Colin and another fellow decided to go into business on their own, it was tough at first but they have been successful. I helped a little, knitting and making dresses for Kathryn, and they would visit me when possible. Beth was born September 1st and Colin fetched me to help out while Jan was in hospital. Bill was put into a retirement home in Dipdale near Dudley, and I visited him once a week, doing my shopping on the way home, trying to return the kindness and help he had given me during my troubled years.

The first Christmas without Stan I spent with June (my niece) and family. In the spring Tom came up and took me back with him. He had a beautiful house, built in Corfe Mullen, I stayed with them a fortnight. June 3rd was a Sunday that year, it was my 70th birthday, Colin and family were away on holiday, and I never spoke to anyone all day, the worst birthday I ever had. I went down to Colin's for the children's birthdays and so the year rolled on. I went to June's again for Christmas Day and my family came for New Year. In the February I had a phone call, it was the Matron at Dibdale, telling me that Bill had passed away, and that was the last I heard of Bill.

Now on to more pleasant things, our next holiday was to San Antonio in Ibiza. We were transported to and from the airport by ambulance cars, I never had to lift my case. We stayed at the Arenal, a large hotel right on the beach. I had to share a room with another lady from Dudley, but during the day I went out with Mavis and Sid. Sid had a stroke around the same time as Stan, he could walk around in the hotel, but in his wheelchair when we went out. They were years younger than me but we enjoyed each other's company. One morning we decided to go somewhere different. We had been to the harbour and town so many times we started off in the opposite direction. We found ourselves in open countryside, the road was unmade but completely flat. On one side were olive groves and we passed by tiny detached houses, each had a small garden at the front, full of flowers and surrounded by grape vines, very pretty, never saw any people or traffic. We could see the coastline in the distance so we plodded on, eventually arriving at a small town, and sat outside a small café and enjoyed a welcome cup of tea. A couple came past, I listened, they were speaking in English, so I went after them and asked them if they could tell me the shortest way back to San Antonio. The fellow studied for a moment, it's May 1st, Mayday, the ferry starts today. The took us down to the seafront and showed us where to wait. The beach was deserted, just us three sitting on the jetty, it finally arrived, only a small boat with a motor attached. The lad helped us to get Sid and his chair in and we were away right across the bay, it was better than a two hour walk and Sid loved it.

Now a large garage in Amblecote had given Freda £250 to spend on us on holiday, so it was decided we should go to the races on the Sunday afternoon. She ordered twelve taxis and we all piled in, we had quite a distance to go inland, workmen were repairing the road and as we passed by, the stopped work and took off their berets, they must have thought we were going to a funeral. We arrived at the stadium three hours too early, it was a very hot day so Freda went and asked if we could go inside. It was a very large building and we all found seats overlooking the track. We could hear music and a few of us went to find out what was going on. We went up a wide open staircase and found ourselves looking into a large room full of people. There was a huge cake, seven or eight tiers high, and standing by it a young boy and girl, they looked just like a bride and groom. The girl wore a most beautiful ankle length dress, it was the children's confirmation party. The band started up and dancing commenced, and they beckoned us to come and join them. Freda came up and asked us to leave, she was mad, she said "fancy barging into someone's private party", but we hadn't barged in, they had invited us, and later waitresses came and brought us all a piece of the cake, the musicians came down and joined us and we danced the afternoon away. The racing started at 5pm, it was pony trotting. We had programmes but being in Spanish we couldn't understand a thing. We all had a flutter, Freda took the bets and quite a few of us won. Everybody enjoyed it, the taxis were waiting to take us back, a good day out.

I had another lovely day out with Mavis and Sid, we were walking around the harbour, there was a boat going on a mini cruise, so Mavis asked Sid if we would like to go, he was all for it, so off we went. We left the harbour and we were in open sea, it was very calm and we cruised around the island. We were to have a three hour stay, I have forgotten the name of the place, it was a beauty spot, a small sandy cove and woods coming down almost to the shore. There was just one big restaurant, no problem with the wheelchair as all paths were properly laid. To me it seemed the spot had been landscaped, beautiful trees, shrubs and flowers, we sat under the trees to have our lunch, too hot to go on the beach. We arrived back safely after a lovely peaceful day.

There was a lady in our group who I felt I had met somewhere before, but could not place her until one night sitting inthe lounge the penny dropped. She was the Matron from Dibdale, she didn't remember me at first, I just said Dibdale, "oh yes" she said, "you were Bill's friend", and that was the start of another long friendship. I shared a room with her the next year, we went to Calla Millor in Majorca. It held many memories for me as I had been before with Stan. It's a lovely resort, a nice promenade, we stayed at a big hotel on the sea front. We had two coach tours all around the island, saw the place where South Pacific was filmed and one day I went with another couple by taxi to Palma, the capital, and they dropped us off right outside the Cathedral, we went inside, it was beautiful. I was never one to sit on a beach all day, like to see everything there was to see.

We had a lovely holiday, I have so many memories I am finding it hard to keep everything in perspective. Colin would fetch me for the children's birthdays down in Saffron Walden, Tom and Marj came up for a holiday and took me back with them to Broadstone where I stayed a fortnight. Tom brought me back and took me to see Mrs Seeley, Marj's Mom. I hadn't seen her for years and she asked me to come again one afternoon, so it was arranged and she told me which way to come when I got off the bus. So I went, she lived in a semi-detached bungalow over Pedmore, the doors were open, as a window cleaner was cleaning her porch. Calling her name I walked into her lounge, stopped dead, I was in the wrong house! I apologised to the two old ladies, they begged me to stay and talk to them, apart from the one's son I was the only visitor they had had in the twelve months they had lived there since leaving Birmingham. I stayed for a while and they made me promise to visit them again. Mrs Seeley did laugh when I told her what had happened, but I thought, how strange, I wasn't meant to go to the wrong house, and I kept my promise.

Our next holiday abroad was to Lido di Jesolo in Italy, not very suitable for handicapped people, there's no promenade we had to walk down a side street to the main shopping street and the footpaths were so bad we kept having trouble with the wheelchair. It was lovely on the back of the hotel, a large patio with tables, chairs, swinging hammocks, a swimming pool and you walked right on to a fine sandy beach. All hotels had their own private beach with deck chairs and umbrellas. We had a day out in Venice, a place I had always wanted to see, but I wouldn't care for a holiday there. We also had a trip to Lake Garda and Verona and saw Juliet's balcony and that large open air theatre. A television crew came and photographed us, so we saw ourselves later in the year on the Travel Show.

We had lovely holidays and I was leading a very full life. Colin moved up to Bradford, Jan wanted to live near her family, I was going to visit them and to save Colin having a double journey fetching me, I went by coach from Birmingham. I sat on the front seat, but something seemed to tell me to move further back, which I did. We were on the motorway six miles from Leeds when bang, we had a shattered windscreen and all the glass came into the coach. Police and an ambulance came, the driver was badly cut about the face, and the woman who had taken my seat had glass embedded in her legs. They were both taken to hospital and that could have been me.

Back to more cheerful things. The next year we went to Fuengirola on the Costa Del Sol and stayed in a five star hotel, it was fabulous, the bathroom was all mirrors. I shared the room with Emmie the ex matron. First class entertainment at night, they took us by coach, visiting the various resorts along that coastline. We saw the millionaire's yachts moored in the harbour at Marbella, also visited Nerja, a pretty little village way up in the mountains. It was June 3rd, another birthday, when I went into the dining room for breakfast, everybody was wishing me happy birthday, even people I didn't know. Later all was revealed, unbeknown to me Emmie had stuck a paper on the back of my dress with Birthday Girl written on it. Emmie and I spent the day on the sea front and around the shops, returning to our room late in the afternoon. On our dressing table was a tray with glasses and a bottle of champagne with the compliments of the management, so we invited a few friends and celebrated. This was my last holiday with the handicapped.

Colin kept in touch with me, rang every Sunday night, and they would come and stay with me, whenever possible, the children loved to come. It was coming up to Christmas again, the phone rang, it was my youngest granddaughter Beth, "Hello Grandma, you have a birthday next year", so I said I hope so, "Well" she said, "You will be in America". She was so excited I couldn't understand what she was talking about, colin came to the phone and explained, he had booked for us all to go to Florida at the end of May, all I needed was spending money. We were to fly from Manchester, so he fetched me two days before. We had to be up at 3am to get the coach at 4.30am to the airport, the flight was 8.45am. Then it was announced there would be a long delay owing to a technical fault in the plane, so we took the children to the play area. Later there was a bomb scare, Police came, everybody had to be moved out of the area. Jan was frantic, tried to get to the children, they prevented her, saying they would be quite safe where they were being taken, it was a worry.

It was some time before we had the all clear. They gave us two free meals as it was 6.45pm before we got away. After a five hour flight we landed at Bangor on the border with Canada, we had to get off while they refuelled and checked the plane. It was 2.30am when we finally got to our hotel. Colin got the keys, opened the door to my room, only to find a young couple in bed, the fellow jumped out of bed, we apologised, they had given us the wrong key. What a start to a holiday. No more mishaps, I had my 75th birthday in the Magic Kingdom, we had three days there, its wonderful, so much to see and do. We visited Sea world, Epcot and the NASA space Centre. We spent the week in Orlando, then on to Fort Lauderdale for the second week. It's a beautiful resort, we stayed at the Yankee Trader on the sea front, and beautiful white sandy beaches, but it was too hot for the children to go on as it was ninety degrees. Colin hired a car for three days. We went to an Indian settlement and it was quaint to see their way of life. Colin said he would like to get down to Key West, so we started off early one morning. I remember going through Miami, so many lines of traffic on the highway and having to drive on the opposite side of the road and traffic lights up in the air, it was scary.

We got down to the start of the Everglades and there were large alligators swimming in the water at the side of the road. After so long Colin realised we were not going to make it to Key West so at the first opportunity we turned back. We stopped for a break, followed a path through some trees and came to a small bay, it was pretty. Jan and I sat under a coconut tree, they were growing on the beach, it must have been a popular place as there were proper toilets. Colin and the girls played around in the sea. Another day I treated them to a trip on a large paddle steamer, around the waters of Lauderdale where the millionaires have their mansions. We were told they have to pay £300 a day just to moor their boats. We had a wonderful holiday.

I had been to places and saw sights I would never see again but I have lots of snaps to remind me. The next two years I went with Jack and Jose, travelled by coach to Santa Susanna on the Costa Brava. It was only six miles from Blanes and I was thrilled to see that little town again where Stan and I had spent so many holidays. We planned to go again the next year but when Jack came to pick me up he told me I was going on my own. The previous night Josie had a fall and broke a bone in her foot. I didn't want to go on my own but when he put my case in the coach I had no option. The journey wasn't very pleasant, but as soon as I got to the hotel I made friends. While waiting for my key in reception there were two elderly ladies and gentlemen sitting near me, trying to sort out their money. So I asked if I could help them, so started a friendship which lasted through my holiday. They were two sisters, Doris and Benny, and James was Benny's man friend, I had all my meals with them, but during the day Doris and I went out on our own, so what started out as a disaster turned out quite pleasant.

We went again the next year, we loved the place. It was Wednesday, half our holiday over, we had lounged about all day, we went up to get washed and changed ready for dinner. I told Jose I would wait in the coffee lounge. We still had time to spare when they came down so we decided to go round the shops. As soon as I got outside I felt queer, I went so hot, couldn't get my breath and dropped down on a seat. I didn't go to dinner and went to bed. I started having pains across my chest, Josie came to me several times during the night, I didn't want to worry her, told her I was alright. The pain eased off towards the morning, I didn't go in for breakfast. I knew there was a chemist next door to the hotel so I went to see if they could recommend something. She told me to go back and ask them to call a doctor. He came, took my blood pressure, tested my heart and said ???? you. Medic spoke broken English, from there I was taken to St Juan hospital in Callela, put on a heart machine and then put to bed in a private ward. No use asking questions, except for the doctor nobody spoke English. Josie came to see me on the Friday and she found the doctor, who told her they would fly me home on the Monday. She could go home with me and there would be an ambulance waiting at Birmingham airport to take me to Russell's Hall.

So she said she would go back and pack our cases, and Jack could take them back home on the coach. He left the next day, Saturday, as our holiday was finished. Jose came on the Sunday afternoon and the doctor told her the airline refused to take me until 14 days had elapsed, she would be allowed to stay at the hotel. I was in bed on adrip for two days, when that was taken off I was able to walk around, but I couldn't hold a conversation with anybody, nobody spoke English. It was a beautiful hotel, I had my own bathroom, a balcony overlooking the town and the sea in the background. I was discharged the following Friday and back at the hotel for another week, of course everything had gone back home. I only had the clothes I had gone to the hospital in, a nighty and dressing gown. Jose had got in touch with Jack, there would be a holdall on the coach arriving Saturday morning. He sent me a pile of pants but only one blouse, and a letter with Colin's phone number asking me to phone him Sunday night. Saturday was my 80th birthday. We tried all night to get Colin, the lines were jammed, next morning I went to a telephone exchange just down the road, they got through for me. Was I glad to speak to him and convince him I was alright, it must have been a very worrying time for him. He said he would be at the airport when I returned home. So Jose and I spent a restful but pleasant week. A taxi was booked to take us to Barcelona airport, it cost me £40, when we went to the desk to check in, our flight hadn't been paid for, a worry we could have done without, we went and sat down, wondering what we could do. After a time, they called us over to the desk, they had phoned our insurance brokers in England and were given the OK. We travelled back Club, which is first class, and served a two course meal. Colin and the girls were waiting for me when we landed, I made a good recovery.

I no longer went to the Evergreen Club or Salvation Army, instead I went to the Carlisle Hall in Stourbridge four days a week for lunch, and I joined their friendship club, making a lot of new friends, a dancing class was held on Friday afternoon. I went on a day trip to Blackpool with them for just £2. Ada (my new friend) and I went with them to Great Yarmouth for a tinsel and turkey holiday. We had free Christmas lunch and day trips during the Summer, and Colin's family would come and stay with me during the school holidays.

I was leading a full happy life, but it wasn't to last. It was ten days before Christmas, I had finished my lunch, went to get up, a pain shot down my right leg. I was in agony, I couldn't put my foot to the ground, Hartley brought me home by car. Val (a friend) happened to be passing, came in and phoned for the doctor, if I could get down for 5 o clock he would see me, otherwise he would come the next day. I rang Jose and asked if Jack would take me to the doctors. They both came but couldn't get me down the front steps, so they rang for an ambulance, as the pain was getting worse. Paramedics came and said if they took me to Russell's Hall I would have to wait at least three hours so they rang the doctor. He said I had a trapped sciatica nerve and would call again the next day and left me strong painkillers. At 9pm I rang Colin, told him what had happened and he said he would be with me around midnight. He arrived, made us drinks and I told him to go to bed. I never got undressed, he made me comfortable in the armchair and I stayed all night.

Next morning Colin got in touch with Social Services, the administrator came, promised to give me all the help she could, but would I think about going into a home. I knew Colin couldn't stay with me long, so I consented. The doctor came, he said he would like me to have my spine X rayed, so he ordered an ambulance. Meantime Mrs Marshall came back with a wheelchair, walker and a night commode. Colin had got a single bed down into the lounge. She had also reserved me a place in Rosemary Smith's retirement home, should it be necessary. We had to wait three hours before they called me in for the X ray, they gave me hell, they caught hold of my bad leg to pull me over on to my stomach, I screamed with pain. Back with Colin he fetched drinks and sandwiches, we had got to wait for an ambulance to come from Stafford. I was Taken to Rosemary's, it was 10pm and they got me into bed, I was past caring what happened to me. Colin drove home that night, leaving my house keys with Margaret, my niece, who bought me clothes and whatever I needed. It was Christmas next weekend and Colin said he would fetch me home as they would come and stay for ten days, but I had made myself so comfortable I decided to stay. I had so many visitors, Colin and the girls came every day but Jan went down with flu and had to keep away. Colin arranged for an osteopath to visit me, he came four times and massaged my leg and gave me acupuncture. I really enjoyed my Christmas, the carers were so good and it's such a pleasant home, I was there for three weeks and Colin took me home. Carers came in the morning, got me washed and dressed, then at night to get me ready for bed and a tray, with a flask of hot water, a cup, tea bag, sugar and milk in case I needed a drink during the night or early morning. Dinners were delivered from the Carlisle Hall four days a week. It took twelve months to get mobile again and it's now two years since it happened, and I am now eighty four years old. I still have the carers come in one day a week for a wash down and they do my work, my washing is no problem. I have an automatic and tumble drier. I can get on and off buses so I do my own shopping. I realise I am doing very well for my age. Writing this I feel I have lived my life again, many happy memories, sad ones too, and I shall try to enjoy what time I have left.

There's a saying "We know not what the future holds, the year's are wisely veiled"

How true.

Ellen's Family

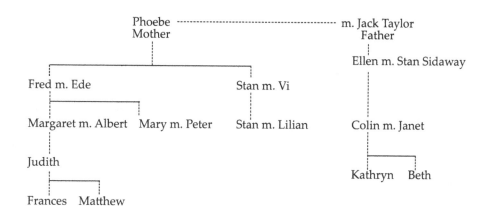

Stan Sidaway's Family

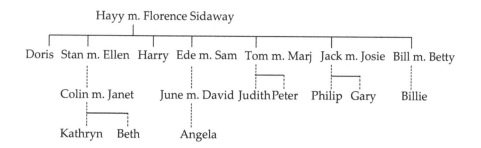